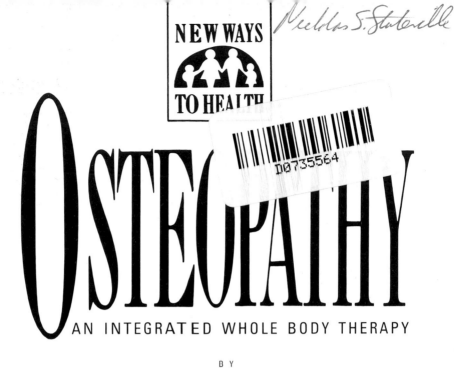

NEW WAYS TO HEALTH

OSTEOPATHY

AN INTEGRATED WHOLE BODY THERAPY

BY

STEPHEN SANDLER, D.O., M.R.O.

FOREWORD BY

DOMENICK J. MASIELLO, M.A., D.O.

PREFACE BY

JOHN E. UPLEDGER, D.O., F.A.A.O.

OF THE

UPLEDGER INSTITUTE
OF HOLISTIC HEALTHCARE

HARMONY BOOKS
NEW YORK

Published by Harmony Books, a division of Crown Publishers, Inc., 225 Park Avenue South, New York, New York 10003.

Originally published in Great Britain in 1989 by The Hamlyn Publishing Group Limited, a division of the Octopus Publishing Group.

HARMONY and colophon are trademarks of Crown Publishers, Inc:

Produced by Mandarin Offset
Printed and bound in Hong Kong

Library of Congress Cataloging-in-Publication Data

Sandler, Stephen.
    Osteopathy: An Integrated Whole Body
    Therapy
    (New Ways to Health)
    Bibliography: p.
    Includes Index.

    1. Osteopathy – Popular works.
    I. Title. II. Series.
    RZ344.S26 1989
    615.5'33

88-16589

ISBN 0–517–57146–3

10 9 8 7 6 5 4 3 2 1

First Edition

Editorial Note
He or she. We have followed the sex of the author and the practitioner in the photographs when frequent referral to the practitioner is neccessary in the text. Of course the profession is open to both sexes.

Publisher's Note
This book is designed as a source guide for readers to use when deciding to participate in an overall osteopathic program. The decision to seek health advice from an osteopath is individual choice.

CONTENTS

FOREWORD

Although *Osteopathy: An Integrated Whole Body Therapy* is written from the perspective of a British osteopath, it provides a relevant introduction to this traditional American healing art. Differences between American and British practice are well documented and osteopathy is placed in proper context with relation to the history of medicine and current related therapies. Both the philosophical and scientific foundations of osteopathy are discussed. The book's strength, however, lies in its case histories and highly practical illustrations of osteopathy's usefulness with children and adults, pregnant women, the newborn, the elderly, athletes, the disabled, and dental patients.

No mere technique or therapy, osteopathy is a way of viewing illness, health, and life itself from a holistic perspective. Although the musculoskeletal system is used as its basic approach to the patient, osteopathy's range of action includes all body systems. Practiced in its pure form, osteopathy can stimulate profound change on the physical, mental and emotional levels, placing its clinical efficacy on a par with classical homeopathy and traditional acupuncture.

Osteopathy, with its rich 115-year history of preventive medical care, provides an alternative to the shortcomings of high technology, crisis management medicine. Regrettably, only a small minority of the approximately 28,000 American osteopathic physicians currently utilize their training in manipulation. The challenge for the osteopathic profession in the future will be to rededicate itself to its holistic roots and offer the American public easily accessible traditional osteopathic care. It is hoped that this volume will stimulate the already growing interest in alternative medical care and motivate the consumer to demand from the medical establishment the freedom to choose a drugless form of therapy.

Domenick John Masiello, MA, DO

PREFACE

Osteopathy was founded in America in 1874 by Andrew Taylor Still and in Britain in 1915 by John Martin Littlejohn, one of Still's graduate students. Since then, in order to gain equal recognition under law, osteopathy has developed as a parallel system of medicine in America, with specialisms in every medical field from dermatology to psychiatry as well as in osteopathic principles and manipulative therapy itself. This means that a DO qualified physician may not necessarily offer osteopathic care in its truest sense, with its emphasis on the body as a self-healing and regulating unit and its use of osteopathic manipulation to help body structure problems that can impair this function.

This situation can be confusing to patients seeking osteopathic care. I believe that it is best for patients first to become familiar with osteopathic principles so that they can decide how osteopathy can help them – and this book offers a good introduction. Stephen Sandler provides an accessible, in depth view of the application of osteopathic principles to a wide range of problems focusing on the treatment of the musculoskeletal and related systems by osteopathic manipulation. The situation in the consulting room, as it affects the patient, is described and illustrated from case history, structural examination, diagnosis and treatment techniques.

The best way to find a suitable osteopathic physician is often to ask friends or colleagues. Alternatively, you can get a recommendation from one of the osteopathic colleges or from the American Academy of Osteopathy, and the book provides advice and information on this. There are also quite a few osteopathically oriented MDs, some of whom may be found through holistic medical societies, or, again, by word of mouth. We are in a state of healthcare transition at the moment and as interest in holistic medicine grows there is an encouraging resurgence in the principles of osteopathy which crosses professional boundaries. I hope *Osteopathy: An Integrated Whole Body Therapy* will provide greater practical understanding of the osteopathic approach to healthcare.

John E. Upledger, D.O., F.A.A.O., D.Sc.
Palm Beach Gardens, Florida

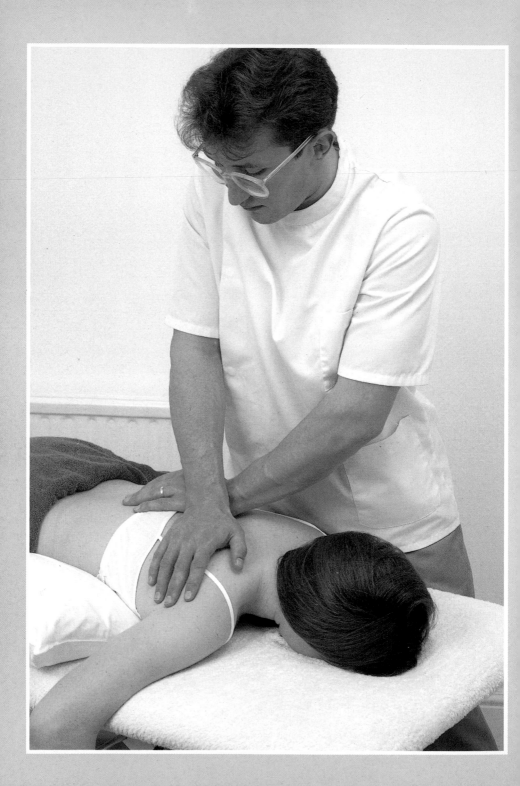

1

INTRODUCTION

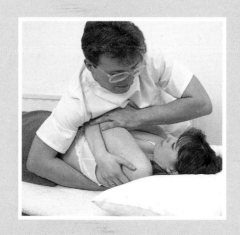

Osteopathy is a 'whole body' system of health care. As an alternative (or complement) to orthodox medicine, osteopathy defines its subject as the whole person. It takes into account not only physical symptoms, but also the patient's lifestyle and attitudes, and his or her overall health. It seeks to treat the patient as a whole, considering mental, physical and emotional factors simultaneously, rather than as a collection of body systems that can be treated more or less in isolation from each other.

Osteopaths are able to diagnose reductions in function and to treat the entire structure of the body to improve health. At the same time, osteopathy looks after the workings of the body as a single and very complex organism, rather than as a collection of components.

Holism

In recent years the word 'holism' has come into common usage in a medical context. It is frequently said that osteopathy, like other 'alternative' methods of health care, is 'holistic' and the concept of holism is worth examination.

The term 'holism' comes from the Greek *holos*, meaning whole. It was coined in 1926 by the South African statesman Jan Smuts, in his philosophical work *Holism and Evolution*. In simple terms, holism encapsulates the view that 'the whole is greater than the sum of its parts'. When a complex thing is taken to pieces and broken down into its constituent parts, it loses its identity. All the parts are there, but they in no way resemble the thing they become when they are linked together. Equally, when the pieces are put back together, they cease to be components and merge together, becoming something entirely new and complete in itself.

Osteopathy and holism

Andrew Taylor Still (1828-1917), the founder of osteopathy, was swimming against the scientific tide when, in the nineteenth century, he pronounced the holistic view that 'the body is a unit'. By this, he meant that each tiny part of the body and, in turn, each of its systems, is intimately connected to every other part and every other system. When the function of any part of the body is less than 100 per cent, the rest of the body is affected in some way or another.

His view of the body made a stark contrast to the way in which established medical science was concentrating on particular diseases and treating the symptoms that they manifested. Patients who came to a doctor with a cough were often viewed merely as a pair of lungs and a windpipe (or a respiratory system), and patients with duodenal ulcers were seen as a digestive tract (or a gastro-intestinal system). To Still and his early followers, however, it was vitally important that they never ignored the fundamental principle that, no matter what part of the body showed signs of illness or injury, every other part of the body was affected.

The holism of Still's formulation of osteopathy in the nineteenth century remains today in marked contrast to the 'systems approach' of much of modern medical thinking.

And it is central to osteopathy as whole–body approach to health care.

Andrew Taylor Still (1828-1917).

Structure and function

On a more practical level, a second principle of osteopathy is that structure governs function. That is, the body can only function at optimum levels if it is structurally sound. Alteration in the structure of the body (especially the spine) leads to reduced or impaired function in its organs and tissues.

A good example of structure governing functioning can be found in the operation of nerves. A nerve is covered with a fine membrane that contains hundreds of minute blood vessels, keeping it supplied with oxygen and other essential nutrients. It must act as both a wire to conduct impulses to and from the brain, and as a conduit, through which oozes, very slowly, a steady stream of thick jelly-like fluid. If a nerve is squeezed, twisted or stretched beyond a certain point, it begins to malfunction. It sends out random signals in all directions, to the confusion of the rest of the nervous system. In addition, when the impulses that the nerve is supposed to conduct reach the trouble spot, they are blocked. The altered structure of the nerve has altered the way in which it functions, causing repercussions in the rest of the body.

By paying attention to the overall significance of any alteration in structure or function, an osteopath is able to interpret whole patterns of aches, pains and general health problems that other eyes might regard as unconnected.

Osteopathy's manual approach to the diagnosis and treatment of patients also enables the practitioner to go one step further. By careful assessment and interpretation of results, the osteopath can not only analyse a patient's problem, but is also able to suggest why the condition has arisen and what can be done to help.

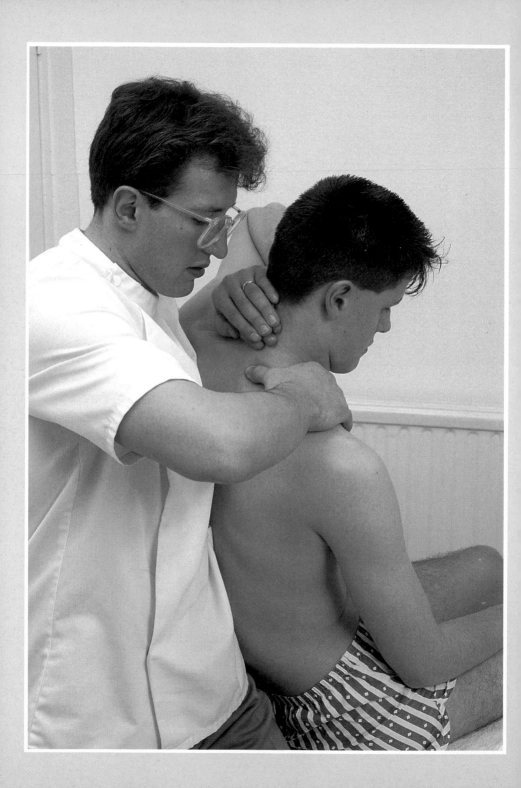

2

HOW CAN OSTEOPATHY HELP?

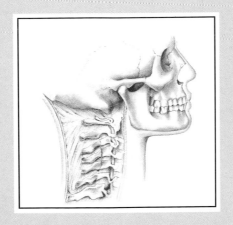

For anyone thinking of consulting an alternative practitioner, the important question is the same. Whatever the therapy – acupuncture, homeopathy, osteopathy, or anything else – everyone wants to know, quite rightly, 'How can it help me?'

There are lots of ways of talking about this. Let's take the time to go into some detail about exactly what illness and health are, and where osteopathy can help change the first into the second.

What does it mean to be really well, full of health? There are all sorts of ways in which scientists, conventional medical practitioners and, for that matter, osteopaths try to describe good health. One of the favourites is to say it's like a well-designed, well-maintained machine that runs sweetly and smoothly. Another is to say it's like a perfect specimen of a beautiful tree – let's say an oak – which has a wonderfully balanced array of branches, nothing broken or missing, and not a single blemish. Some would say that full health is like 'the ideal picture' or 'the ideal piece of music' – everything perfectly balanced and harmonized.

In fact, however, there is no substitute for the real thing. Just think of a child that you know, about two to three years old, standing in front of you with shining eyes, healthy skin and hair and an excited face, just bursting with energy and life. That is optimum health personified. Most of us, happily, are as healthy as this for at least part of our lives, before the stresses and cares and worries get to us in later years.

The World Health Organization defines health quite simply, as follows:

> Health is a state of complete physical, mental and social
> well-being, not merely the absence of disease or infirmity.

This fits in quite well with our picture of the child who is just 'raring to go'. It also includes the idea, which we will follow up in detail later on, that a healthy body and a healthy mind go together and depend on each other. It is in comparison with this that likening a healthy person to a machine falls short. The machine that truly thinks and feels has not yet been invented! Furthermore, living things can also do something quite remarkable, which machines cannot do at all: they can repair themselves of even quite severe and complicated damage. It is the human body's remarkable capacity for self repair that is the centre of the osteopath's philosophy.

The bloom of good health is unmistakable. Health is not merely the absence of illness but the full realization of potential, like a mature tree in full leaf.

The self-repairing body

The founder of osteopathy based much of his teaching on the principle that the body is very good at looking after itself. Osteopathy is the method he developed to deal with the structural malfunctions and misalignments that prevent the body from doing its proper job of healing and repair.

We all know the body has this ability, and when we see it written or hear it said we think 'So what?' But isn't it amazing how quickly we forget, when we don't feel well? The body's capacity for healing itself is then frequently abandoned in favour of something to make us feel better immediately.

Carefree children on holiday are joie de vivre *personified. Their young, flexible bodies are still growing, and have not yet been fixed into adult postures dictated by job, environment and habit.*

Think of how quickly and efficiently our bodies deal with damage, from a small cut to a cracked or broken bone. The wound is systematically sealed off and made safe, and then the damaged tissue is repaired. The same progression is followed when there is a more general threat to our health, such as infection or a mild bout of food poisoning. This time the body marshals resources from a wider area, and again directs them toward combating the source of the problem. Our entire system acts as a unit to protect, repair and heal itself.

But if the body – our body – is so good at looking after and healing itself, why do we have such complex systems of medical care? What is it that hinders the body's repair mechanisms to such an extent that each year huge amounts of money are spent on health care? The answers to these questions lie in our understanding of how someone becomes 'unwell', and how slight 'unwellness' develops into 'ill health'.

In most cases, illness does not strike out of the blue. A little research indicates that it is almost always the result of a long history of tiny, seemingly significant occurrences. We regard it as old age creeping up on us; most people do not regard themselves as ill, or malfunctioning, at all. Nevertheless, to an osteopath – and many other medical specialists – these little details build up into what is known as a 'disease picture'.

To illuminate this, let us take a hypothetical example and trace an imaginary person's life from childhood to middle age, using postural development as an illustrative example of how and why things can go wrong. Then we will examine how osteopathy can help both with urgent needs and with the long-term problems that brought about the crisis.

Sam, a suitable case for treatment

The subject of our hypothetical case is called Sam. The study begins when he is five years old, 'learning his lessons' at school. But in the previous five years many, many things have been learned already. He's progressed from being a small bundle of relatively unco-ordinated bits and pieces at birth. He has learned how to walk and talk, how to stand still, to run, and to sit and eat.

Like most people, Sam has learned all of these things from his family. We all learn from our mothers and fathers if we are the first child, and from our brothers and sisters as well if we are one of several children. All children watch and listen carefully to the things that the people around them say and do – and imitate them, often with devastating accuracy.

So in many ways Sam will have imitated and copied his family in their funny little ways. Most families have quirks of posture that pass through generations. The best place to spot these is in wedding or other family photographs: sometimes you'll see a whole group of people who always cock their heads to one side. In Sam's case his father is an inveterate 'lounger' – he always stands with most of his weight on one leg, and holds the other knee bent. Because of this his pelvis drops to one side and his spine takes on a long, gentle

We all have postural quirks — heredity and force of habit have shaped our bodies — and these faults often make matters worse for us later in life and when we injure ourselves. Osteopaths are trained to spot such bad habits as perpetual lounging, (the 'gossip posture') where all the weight is thrown onto one leg.

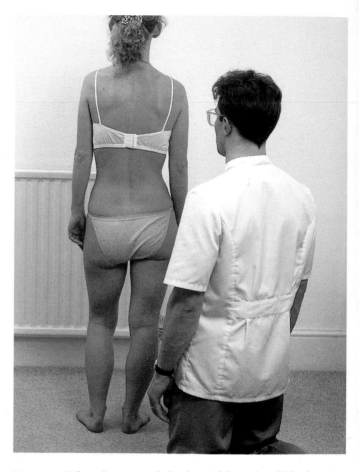

S-curve. Often these people look as if they should be leaning against a lamp post, or perhaps a garden wall. This may be why this position is sometimes referred to as 'the gossip posture'.

This posture is already the centrepiece of Sam's repertoire of postures. He copies his father, his elder brother and his sister in other ways too, such as holding his arms when he's talking, but his use of the gossip posture is the one that interests us. As the years go by, he persistently stands with most of his weight on his left leg, and his right leg flexed at the knee. Sometimes he puts his right toe on the ground — and when he is in this particular position we are interested in the fact that the powerful set of muscles at the back of his thigh, the hamstrings, are shortened and not used properly.

For a muscle to be in tiptop shape it needs to be used regularly. As far as a muscle is concerned, 'regular use' means a combination of full stretch and strong work. This particular set of muscles is used for walking, running and jumping, as well as for standing in the erect position — square on two feet.

When the group of muscles on one side of the body is used differently from that on the other they develop accordingly. In this case it is likely that the hamstring on the right side, frequently being held in a short position, will, over a period of years, become less elastic than it should be, and less elastic than its counterpart on the left.

A similar problem affects many people after a leg injury — osteopaths often observe it in amateur skiers, who have developed it as a result of breaking a leg. After the leg has been in a plaster cast for six to ten weeks, all of the muscles on that side are 'wasted'. That is, they have become weak, and lose their bulk and firmness. Regular therapy and exercise is needed to bring the muscles back to the kind of condition they should be in, or the body will find ways to adapt to having a weak

Downhill racing may be exhilarating, but the inexperienced or unlucky may be brought home in plaster at the end of the day. Osteopathic manipulation cannot cure a broken leg, but it can help to restore muscle tone and strength when the plaster comes off to prevent permanent postural damage that may be caused as the body compensates for the temporarily weak limb.

component and they'll possibly never recover. On the other hand, the process can be highly accelerated, as we see in the cases of professional sportsmen for whom full fitness is their urgent preoccupation.

During Sam's school career, this has no noticeable significance. This is primarily because schoolchildren are very active for at least some time in every day. Children are also more adaptable than adults and marginal, hardly perceptible asymmetries cause the body no immediate trouble.

A significant thing about childhood years, however, is that patterns set and established at that time of life continue for many years. The gentle pull of the muscles above and below the pelvis, the large hip bones, gradually works its way into those bones and into the spine. As time passes, a very slight twist – called a torsion or spiral (otherwise known as a scoliosis) – will be established in the bones, the ligaments and

Children are lithe and adaptable, flexible and highly mobile. It is important that their whole bodies get as much exercise as possible to prevent any bad postural habits from developing.

other sets of muscles along the way. Very often the whole skeleton shows a twist of this kind from top to bottom, which can be seen if the person is looked at from above when they are standing.

By the time Sam leaves school, at 18, and goes to college, all of these trends are firmly established. Fortunately, Sam is a keen sportsman; he is a skilful soccer player and a good tennis player. While he's at college – studying art and design – he continues to attend regularly at the gym as well as playing sports. But in the college bar in the evenings he still stands in that same old way – left knee straight, right knee bent. Obviously, playing two fairly rugged sports he's had a few knocks, and he has twisted his left ankle quite severely on two occasions.

At this stage he's young enough, and unconcerned enough, to have let his ankle heal over a few days of 'taking it easy'. He hasn't noticed that each time he's had to keep his weight off his painful sprained left ankle he seems to have been mildly troubled by an aching back.

We can guess, from our knowledge of his history, that this might be linked to his sudden need to change from standing one way to standing another. We might even wonder whether his left ankle is vulnerable precisely because it does so much work when he stands around working or chatting.

Whatever the reason, Sam accepts the small discomforts he feels occasionally; he is so concerned with getting his ankle right for Saturday's game that he doesn't really bother about his backache.

By the time he's 25, he has a job, a house, and he has married. He works quite a long day, mostly standing at a drawing-board. He sometimes has to attend conferences – standing a lot and chatting – and there's also the occasional presentation of new work to clients and customers. He does sometimes use a draughtsman's stool-cum-chair but even when sitting (although he's only vaguely aware of this) he is more comfortable with the right side of his bottom off the seat and all his weight put through his left side.

He still enjoys a game of tennis, but plays less frequently now. On Sundays he likes to play soccer for his local side, but training sessions are few and far between. Occasionally he feels guilty about losing fitness and takes more regular exercise for a while. When this happens, although he's not a heavy smoker, he cuts out cigarettes altogether. He also reduces his alcohol intake. He takes these steps because he has a vague idea that they improve his general health.

Sam at 30

Now that he's approaching 30, still happily married and with two small children, it's a good time to assess his level of health, and to predict where things may go wrong in the years ahead.

To an osteopath, posture is the key to understanding a person's general physical state. In Sam's case, it is easy to see how his childhood posture has developed if his body is viewed from the back. With this rear view, it is obvious just how lopsided Sam has become – and he's still only 30. One shoulder higher than the other, and his head is held to one side. This is a natural extension of the S-curve configuration of his spine. His pelvis is tilted and the muscles of his left and right thigh have noticeably different bulk. Look also at how his left foot has collapsed under the strain of carrying nearly twice as much weight as it would normally have to do if he stood evenly.

Less obvious, but equally significant, is the state of his thorax – the ribs and breastbone. To fit in with the curves in his spine, the ribs of his right side have been squeezed together.

The feet take the brunt of bad posture, not always uncomplainingly. Sometimes the arches collapse under the strain of the extra weight they carry because the body is out of balance. Osteopathy can help with foot problems.

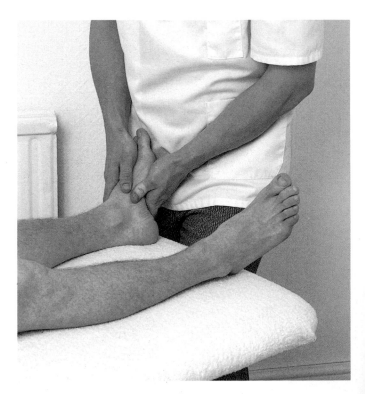

SAM FROM BEHIND

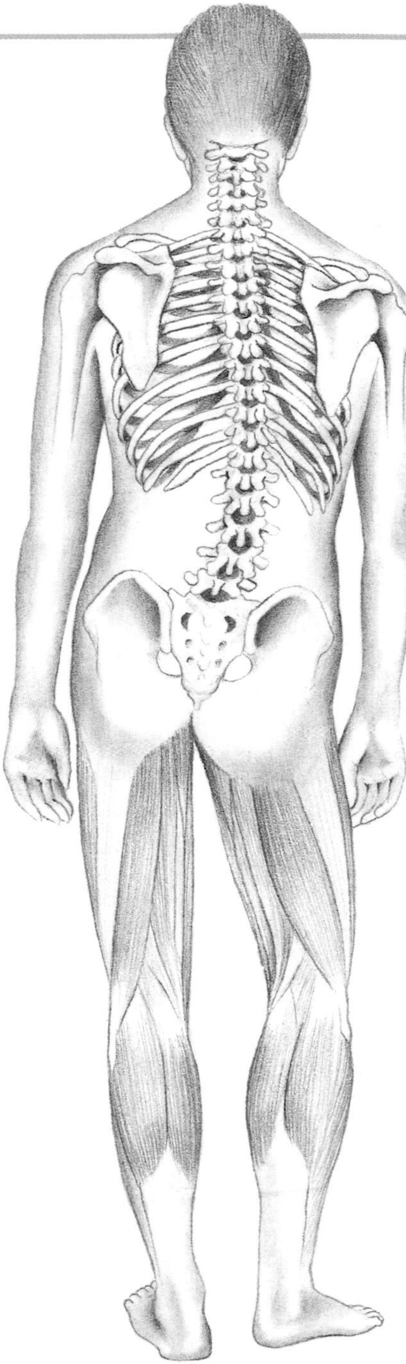

one shoulder
higher than
the other

ribs spread out

S-shaped curve
to spine

different bulk in
muscles of left
and right thigh

weight transferred
to left side

ankle ligaments
very weak

arch of left foot
collapsed under
the strain

shoulder pushed
forward

ribs crowded,
restricting
breathing

pelvis tilted

hamstrings
shortened

right knee flexed
while standing

back view

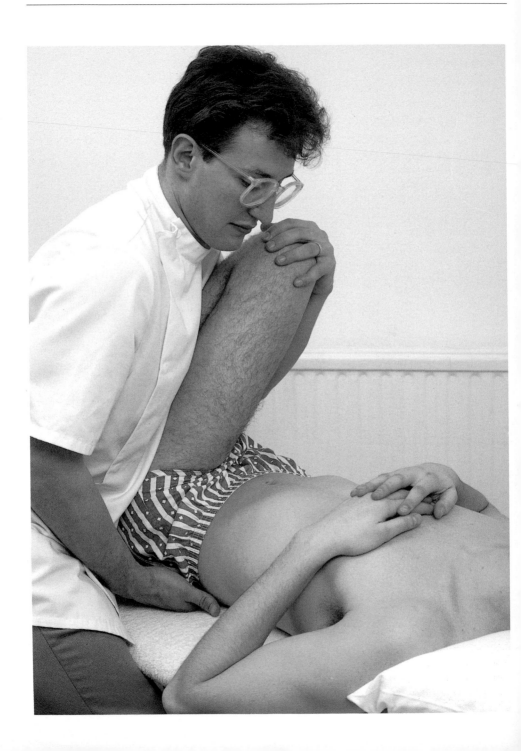

This means that when he breathes, his respiratory movements are distorted. As he breathes in, the ribs on the left have less room to separate because they've already been opened up by the curvature, while the ribs on the right are crowded together and have less freedom of movement. Also, when we look at his right leg, which has spent a good deal of the past 30 years half flexed, we can see that it doesn't like being straightened fully. The hamstrings, together with the strong muscle and ligament down the outside of the thigh, normally hold the knees slightly flexed, so that when each knee is straightened it is under tension. This leads to the knee being bent to the side, rather in the way a tight bowstring maintains the curve in a bow.

Sam also has a problem developing in his shoulders. As we have seen, he holds his right shoulder lower than his left. Because he uses his right hand a lot when working at his drawing-board, over the years he has developed a tendency to push his right shoulder forward. He also works with his head tilted to the left. These two things together have had a marked effect on the many muscle groups that anchor and control the head and arm. The result is that the freedom of movement of his shoulders is restricted – the right especially so when he pulls it back. He also has quite different ranges of movement of his head to the left and to the right. This is associated with the tensions in the muscles in the back of his neck. In just the same way that his hamstrings have developed differently in each thigh, so have the neck muscles grown differently on either side. An important distinction, however, is that the distortion of the neck muscles has occurred as a result of the studying and the artwork he has done in the last 12 years, whereas the uneven development of the legs has been in progress for a lifetime.

The twist of the neck does not just affect the muscles there; it also has significance for the brain, which relies on getting enough blood in order to work. Some of that blood reaches the brain through a vessel called the vertebral artery, which actually winds through holes in the bones that make up the top six vertebrae of the spine. This is designed to protect the vulnerable supply line, but it does mean that where the bone goes, the artery has to go too. When the head is held tucked to one side for long periods of time, there is a possibility that the artery will begin to behave a bit like an old hose pipe and develop a kink. Someone of 30 is unlikely to have any problem

A great deal is expected of the sacro-iliac joint, which joins the pelvis to the backbone at the base of the spine. It transmits the weight of the body to the legs. It has very little mobility, and is almost entirely supported by ligaments, with very little help from the muscles. It is therefore very vulnerable and the source of much low back pain.

Osteopaths will examine the joint by palpation (feeling with the hands) as a routine part of any consultation, and can apply many techniques to treat it if there is a problem.

THE VERTEBRAL ARTERY

The vertebral artery threads its way through a tunnel of vertebrae on the way to the brain. If the vertebrae are out of alignment, the artery may kink, disrupting the blood supply to the brain.

side view

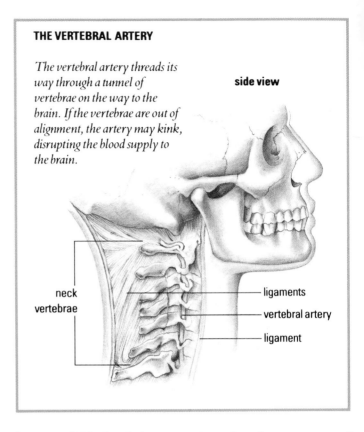

neck vertebrae

ligaments

vertebral artery

ligament

because of this, but in later years it can be a frequent cause of intermittent giddiness.

Sam is sometimes painfully aware of his neck when he wakes in the morning. He always puts this down to having slept heavily, or to overdoing things the day – or the night – before. He hasn't yet realized that when he adopts a certain position on his left side, or on his front, he puts a considerable strain on those tight, stringy muscles on the left side of his neck. Furthermore, when he sleeps deeply he doesn't register the early signs of discomfort and move around to minimize them.

During a normal night's sleep most people move from one position to another almost all the time, spreading the weight of the head and body over different muscles and ligaments, sharing the load. In contrast, if Sam sleeps heavily, he usually wakes feeling aches and stiffness, combined with a sense of being mentally sluggish.

This picture of Sam early in his fourth decade makes him seem to be in a bad way. But it's almost certain that if anyone asked him about the level of his health, he would reply, 'Well, I'm not too bad at all, really. I'm not as fit as I was a few years ago, but I'm pretty healthy.'

This contrast between his own view of his health, and the problems we know are developing emphasizes a crucial point. As long as Sam keeps reasonably close to the routine run of things, and as long as nothing untoward happens, he will be all right. Although his body isn't perfect, it can cope with the normal stresses and strains in the system and keep going more or less satisfactorily. Although it is not working at peak efficiency, it is not working so hard that it's in danger of breaking down.

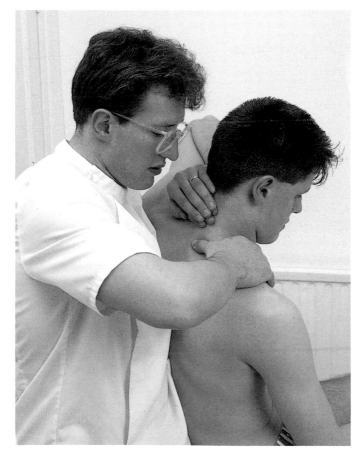

The neck is very mobile whilst the upper back is naturally quite stiff. This is a frequent trouble spot. The osteopath is often called upon to treat this area with manipulation to ease the pain of strains and sprains.

What problems could occur?

A familiar question asked of osteopaths at this point is: 'If a person feels healthy, why should he worry? What sort of problems could occur?' Although there is no easy, catch-all answer, it is possible to say that the trigger is very often something remarkably trivial. Commonly a damaged system such as Sam's, although working quite nicely, is only doing so because it is finely balanced. And because of this it can be upset easily by a small nudge from something that is barely significant in itself. A typical example would be a twisted ankle, for instance.

Suppose Sam goes out walking with his family and some friends. Carrying his youngest child on his shoulders, Sam put his foot in a small hole created by a horse's hoofprint. In the resulting stumble, he twists his left ankle, causing a sharp pain, which becomes a mild ache. Over the next two weeks the ankle pain gradually subsides, but the pain seems to spread to his back, and to the knee on the other side. But he manages to carry on more or less as normal, keeping his weight off the ankle when he stands or walks, and trying to keep the knee as comfortable as possible. The back he just ignores – in the past back pain never lasted long.

By the end of the second week he feels quite well again. Although he's done no more than walk sedately to the train and then into work, he's just about forgotten the problem. But a fortnight later, playing football in the back garden, he feels a sudden stab of pain on the inside of his right knee. By the time he's been helped inside and seated in a chair with his foot up, the pain has changed to a deep, steady throbbing which is quite sickening, and over the next hour the knee swells up considerably. Sam is rather embarrassed, but puts it down to overenthusiasm. He tries to reassure himself: 'it's just a bad ligament sprain – the kind of thing that happens to 33-year-olds who try to kick a ball too hard'.

By the end of the week, Sam is hobbling around on a borrowed walking-stick. But by the middle of the following week he is aware of a growing discomfort in his low back region.

What the osteopath saw

With the in-depth knowledge of Sam's history and condition that our study has given us, we can analyze what has happened and see how an osteopath might look at the problem. First of all, an osteopath would look at Sam's knee.

During all the years of mild misuse, Sam's knee has come to work in an abnormal way. On the inside of his knee, the two main bones are being pulled apart. This means that, given the right circumstances, enough force might be put on the knee to overstretch the ligaments and the muscles in that area.

So, if Sam stands on his left foot and swings his right foot at the ball, he is asking the long hamstring muscles to do two things: to stretch enough to allow his foot to swing forward, and to keep his knee braced. When this problem is added to the fact that he used to be a good soccer player and so uses the *inside* of his foot to kick the ball, thus exerting more force still through that vulnerable inside (medically called 'medial') part

Sitting on top of the world and leading daddy by the nose may be blissful for a child, but if father already has postural problems, such a method of carrying may exacerbate matters.

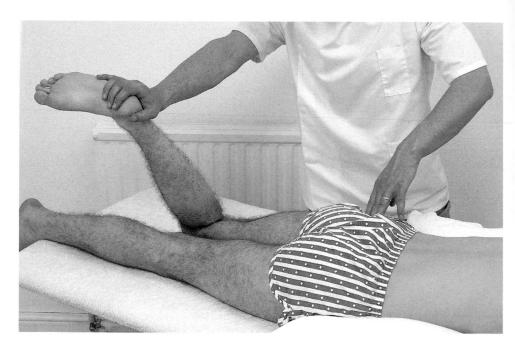

Work on a troubled knee joint will often need complementary work on the hip joint. Deep soft tissue treatment to the buttock will help clear up sciatica, pain along the path of the sciatic nerve which runs from the lower back through the deep muscle of the buttock into the leg.

Here the sacro-iliac joint is examined from the side. It is standard practice for osteopaths to confirm (or revise) diagnosis by examining the patient from several different angles.

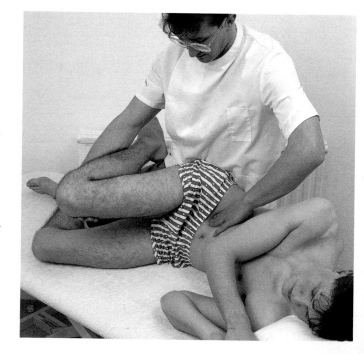

of his knee, we have an overload. The whole thing is already under strain after the injury that occurred two weeks previously.

What would an osteopath do? The answer is of course a number of things, but first the patient's full physical history (as outlined above) would be uncovered; then a treatment plan would be devised. The word 'plan' is especially important, because the treatment will take into account all of the factors contributing to the problem, and tackle them all. Rather than just rubbing the painful spot and trying to alleviate the bruising and inflammation around that ligament and its muscle, the osteopath would assess the damage to the knee, the state of the rest of the lower limb from the foot to the pelvis, and the way the spine and the body work together as a unit. Then the osteopath would make a prediction of what can realistically be expected to change for the better in all of these areas.

As well as working on the knee to reduce the swelling and make it less painful, there would also be work done on the knee joint itself, the hamstrings, the calf muscles, other thigh muscles, the ankle, and the hip, all to help the 'unit' of the lower limb work better. Gradually work would be extended to the low back and the pelvis.

To return to Sam, we find that once again he has been able to 'get by' with a combination of taking it easy, swallowing some pain-killing drugs, and getting friends to drive him to places instead of walking as much as he used to do. He has passed through the most painful stages and has almost managed to return to his normal lifestyle.

The brain and the nervous system are truly amazing in the way they are able to handle pain. According to what circumstances dictate and to what recent memory provides, the brain and the central nervous system control the degree of pain and discomfort arising from any particular physical situation. At some times – examples occur frequently at important sporting occasions – the brain is able to shut off the pain arising from severe damage because the mind considers the task in hand more important. Yet at other times, because the 'memory' of the severe pain of a recent injury is still fresh, the brain will magnify the pain signals coming from a mild new one. It will even sometimes trigger a repeat of the old pain, if it was in the same part of the body or not too great a distance away. Just what this phenomenon means, for Sam and for any osteopath that he might consult, we'll see when his next accident occurs.

The last straw

Since his misadventure with the football, Sam has steered clear of any similar exertion. As a result, his exercise has been confined to gentle strolls to and from work, and a weekly walk with his family. The truth is, however, that anything more than a stroll is painful. Any attempt at brisk walking produces a pain in the back of the knee. This pain radiates into his thigh, his calf, and is followed soon after by an ache in his low back which grows steadily. This is the result of his altered posture and gait, which is exaggerating his long-standing problem. He now walks in a way that reduces the load placed upon his right knee and its muscles. The consequence is that his spine has to contort a little more or do more work when he walks fast or walks for longer than five minutes.

At first this situation is acceptable. But his self-image – how he sees himself – has been shaken by the episode. No longer is he the lithe, fit ex-student who happens to be a working man. He now has to face the fact that he is nearer – as he sees it – to being an overweight, slovenly, middle-aged lump. Understandably, this is not a pleasant prospect.

As the weeks pass, he goes through various stages of mental upheaval, all of which reflect or are reflected in changes in his physical systems. He suffers brief episodes of nausea, indigestion, flatulence, diarrhoea and constipation. He has more headaches than usual and his sleep pattern is disrupted. All of these things are put down to 'stress at work', but in actual fact Sam is finding work more stressful because he is so mixed-up.

One day he decides that it is time for desperate measures, so he buys a mountain bicycle with the intention of doing some serious riding. This, he reasons, will give him fresh air, exercise, and peace and quiet all at the same time. He takes things very sensibly and builds up his riding programme gradually so as not to strain himself.

Unfortunately, one morning he has to swerve quickly off the path to avoid a dog, and falls off the bicycle. Instinctively he puts out his right hand to save himself as he crashes to the ground. Pain shoots everywhere – his knee, his back, his shoulder and his neck. The agony seems totally disproportionate to the minor accident that has caused it. After he picks himself up he feels a stab of pain under his shoulder blades and another in his chest each time he takes a deeper than normal breath. By the time he had wheeled his bike home, Sam was a mass of pain.

A SORRY STATE

The cumulative effects of a succession of minor mishaps are made worse by Sam's fall from his bicycle.

This is what he feels like the day after:

Right knee:	stiff and painful, with pains radiating into the calf and thigh, although there was no bruising and he couldn't remember knocking it.
Low back:	aching, with sharp pains if he makes unguarded movements.
Right Shoulder:	very stiff across the front, mostly near the breastbone.
Chest:	sharp pains at the top with every deep breath.
Neck:	pains all the way down the left side.
Left arm:	an ill defined, tingling sensation down the arm, similar to numbness or 'pins and needles'.
Head:	throbbing headache, with the skin and muscles feeling tender.

He decides to take time off and rest in bed until the pain subsides. After three days of bed rest, with treatment from hot-water bottles acting as hot compresses and pain killing drugs, however, he is not feeling any better, so he asks his wife to drive him to the osteopath a neighbour has recommended.

How an osteopath would help

The details of how an osteopath goes about dealing with a patient will be considered in a later chapter, but initially, Sam needs to know what sort of help he can expect.

All Sam's ailments need to be looked at together, before an osteopath can suggest how he or she could help Sam to get better. It is important that the osteopath thinks in terms of 'helping Sam to get better' rather than 'curing Sam's

HOW THE OSTEOPATH SEES SAM'S CONDITION

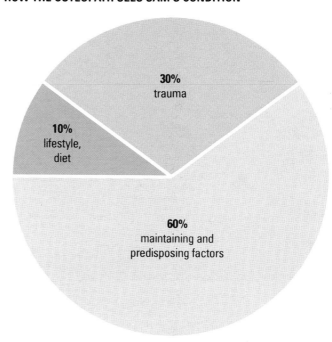

When the osteopath makes his diagnosis, he assesses the proportional effect of environment, lifestyle, diet, heredity, work and injury on his patient's case.

problem'. All of Sam's sufferings have to be put right from within, by his own body – the osteopath merely tries to make it as easy as he or she can for Sam's body to get on with the job.

The osteopath will investigate each damaged tissue and promote the operation of its powers of repair. The pattern that has been there for some years has been badly distorted by sudden stretching and tearing forces. Not only does each mechanical tissue – muscles, ligaments, tendons – have to repair itself, it has to cope with the distortion transmitted through it because of damage elsewhere. These areas of local bruising, spasm and tension can actually form a vicious circle which tends to maintain and prolong the global pattern. Unless change can be induced in one part of this circle, the whole thing can persist for weeks.

The effect of all this pain and stress on the rest of the body can also be considerable, and Sam suffers a recurrence of his bouts of indigestion, breathlessness, and diarrhoea. This happens because of overlapping circuits in the nervous system. The channels carrying the bursts of signals from damaged muscles and joints run close to, and cross over, the nerves which control such functions as sweating, digestion and other 'visceral' functions.

Now is a good point at which to consider how Sam, on the one hand, and his 'environment' (which includes his history and his present circumstances), on the other, can be considered as more easily accessible parts. This is one of the mental processes osteopaths go through when a patient presents them with a problem. It is sometimes termed 'holistic analysis' – because it deals not only with the problem but also, as we have seen, with everything about the patient and the way he or she leads their life.

In order to provide a treatment and management plan, the osteopath will take into account all of these symptoms relating to Sam's internal workings, as well as those relating to his musculo-skeletal system. He or she will put them in the context of Sam's personal and medical histories, his work environment, his posture, his diet, and how he spends his leisure time.

What is vital to the osteopath is to gain an understanding of the state Sam is in, and how he interacts with his environment. He is then able to begin a careful programme designed to help Sam deal with the points of interaction with his environment at which the breakdown and stresses occur. The osteopath uses his hands to examine and treat the physical part of the complex situation. He will also discuss with Sam both how he can modify his behaviour, and what kind of practical changes he can make at home and at work to enable life to go more smoothly.

One way of putting it is that the osteopath is there to enable the patient to get as much out of life as he possibly can, without overdoing it and paying the price of pain and suffering. He may at times complement his own treatment by recommending that a patient consults his family doctor, if appropriate, or a second health care specialist, or he may ask him to make changes in his diet, to follow an exercise programme, or to make adjustments to the chairs, the car, the bed, or even the shoes he uses in order to minimize strain.

Sam, of course, is a hypothetical patient. Yet the sort of holistic analysis summarized here in his case is applied by osteopaths to real patients all the time. Treating the patient's body and mind as a unit, relating it to their way of life, and then taking positive steps to help that unique combination rebalance itself in a more healthy way is the essence of osteopathy.

CASE HISTORIES

ROSEMARY'S RECURRENT KNEE LIGAMENT STRAIN

Rosemary is a 28-year-old hairdresser who is a keen squash player.

Eighteen months ago during a crucial squash game she twisted badly and felt a sharp pain in her right knee. It was bad enough to stop her playing, and to prevent her from driving home. She went along to her family doctor the next morning, but had to be helped to walk because she could not carry any weight on the leg. By this time, the knee was very swollen and she couldn't move it without severe pain.

Her doctor diagnosed strained ligaments and referred her to the local physiotherapy department for ultrasound treatment and exercises. The pain took four weeks to go away, but since then she has had recurrent bouts of pain and stiffness in the knee which has made her give up squash altogether.

She went to see an orthopaedic surgeon who confirmed the diagnosis of torn ligaments but he wanted to operate and so he put her on his waiting list. Rosemary felt that this was not the best solution for her, and therefore she consulted an osteopath to see if there was another approach to the problem.

After taking a full history, the osteopath assessed her total body posture in relation to the knee injury. After eighteen months, her body will be adapting to the injury to a greater or lesser extent which is going to affect the way that the ligaments heal or not. He notices that she is standing with all her weight on her right knee because the right leg is shorter than her left causing her to tilt slightly to one side. She has a spinal curve which confirms this fact.

The osteopath's approach is in two parts. In the short term, he will work on the muscles and ligaments of the knee to encourage draining of the excess fluid and to get the muscles strong enough to support the knee as the ligaments tighten up and heal. The second part of the treatment is to give Rosemary a heel lift in her right shoe, to encourage the weight to be transferred over to the left and away from the bad side thus taking the strain away from the ligaments in the knee as they heal. He also works at the ankle on the right side because it is showing early signs of strain as it has been taking part in a compensation programme for the last eighteen months too. He will also work on the junction areas in the spine with soft tissue and articulation techniques to stretch tissues over the convexity and allow the spine to straighten as much as possible. This approach is designed to lessen the strain on the knee joint.

After four visits, Rosemary finds that she can bend the knee fully without pain and that she runs for about half a mile easily. After another four visits she has had no pain or swelling and the knee feels more stable again. Her spine is more mobile than it was before and she wants to go back to squash. The osteopath encourages her to do this and she is discharged with knee-strengthening exercises that she should do as a routine thing each day and for ten minutes before a squash match as part of her warm up.

CARLO'S WHIPLASH INJURY

Carlo is a 20-year-old office worker. One evening, while waiting in his car at the traffic lights, another car ran into him from behind at about 20mph. Fortunately Carlo's seatbelt prevented him from going through the windscreen. Apart from being shaken up, he felt he was unhurt at the time and so did not think that he needed medical attention.

The next day he awoke with such severe pain and stiffness that any movement of his head caused extreme pain under his skull and down his right arm to the hand.

He phoned the osteopath and was given an appointment for that morning. By the time the osteopath saw him, Carlo's pain was very intense and there was severe muscle spasm. A full examination was not possible. In order to exclude bone damage the osteopath felt that an X-ray was needed and so this was arranged without any further ado. No damage or fracture was found and so in the meantime Carlo was given a collar to wear and some pain-killing tablets.

Carlo rang the osteopath to tell him the good news and a further appointment was arranged for two days' time.

When Carlo arrived for this appointment he was still in a lot of pain but the collar had helped. The examination showed that he had joint locking of the small joints under the skull on both sides together with a severe strain of the musculature; there was also a secondary strain of the joints in the middle of the neck which was responsible for the pain in the right arm.

The osteopath used high velocity thrust techniques designed to break the facet locking of the joints under the skull and this was accompanied by a very loud crack. (He warned Carlo first so that he should not be taken unawares.) The manoeuvre was not without some pain, but it was very fast and done with minimal force and as soon as it had been done the effect was dramatic. There was immediate relief of pain and Carlo could move his head again gently. Now he was treated with gentle traction techniques to calm down the whole area and the osteopath finished with another thrust technique to the lesion lower down to relieve the arm pain. Carlo was told to rest at home for the remainder of the week.

When he was seen again, he felt 90 per cent better with just a little muscle stiffness remaining. At the end of the second treatment he was discharged, with no expectation of further trouble.

JENNY'S ASTHMA

Jenny is a bouncy 9-year-old girl brought to the osteopath by her mother who herself is a patient.

Jenny suffers from asthma, and during an acute attack she has difficulty breathing out which can be very distressing. She has to use a 'puffer' (Ventolin inhaler) and take medication each day; any games or PE at school is out of the question because of the risk of an acute attack. Apart from anything else, Jenny is quite frightened of her asthma and so doesn't want to do PE anyway.

The osteopath looks at Jenny's back and neck muscles as well as her rib and chest muscles because these are what is known as the accessory muscles of respiration and so are involved in the hard work needed to help Jenny breathe. He looks at the diaphragm, the large sheet of muscle that divides the chest from the abdomen, as this is the main muscle of respiration that rises and falls with each breath.

Jenny's osteopath also practises cranial osteopathy, a very gentle approach using the rhythms associated with the supporting tissues of the bones of the head as they expand and contract. This technique also works on the fascia, which is part of the connecting tissue of the body.

He examines her spinal joints to make sure that there are no lesions in the articulations associated with the nervous system that controls the size of the air passages which arise from the chest region of Jenny's spine.

He starts to work on the muscles using a stretch and pull technique known as a muscle energy technique. Children in particular enjoy these techniques, because they can be like games with one person using certain muscles to pull against the other in a very definite but fun way. He also works on the spinal joints to ease strain patterns caused by the fact that the muscles have been working so hard. Occasionally, he uses a cracking or popping technique which doesn't hurt and which makes Jenny giggle.

He asks Jenny's mother about her diet and general health. He finds out that apart from the asthma she suffers from catarrh quite badly, especially in the summer. He prescribes a diet free of all dairy foods for a while because occasionally if a child is allergic to cows' milk this can have an effect on the mucous membranes of the nose and respiratory passages. Goat's milk is tolerated quite well in these circumstances and can be used along with tinned fish as a replacement source of vitamin D.

Jenny is treated twice weekly, and within a month is doing very well indeed. She still has her puffer but is not using it to anything like the same extent. She has more confidence and feels that she would like to start PE at school. Her osteopath is at first reluctant because he feels Jenny is still quite weak and he doesn't want to run the risk of an acute attack which might destroy this new-found confidence.

He extends the treatment interval to one treatment each ten days or so and after another four visits Jenny has not had an acute attack for over a month compared to once a week before the treatment started. Now he feels it will be alright to start PE at school.

Jenny will need treatment on a continuous basis until she has finished growing. This maintenance treatment every two or three months will enable her to live as full a life as possible within the confines of her asthma. She still has her asthma and still needs her medication, but with the osteopath's help can look forward to a better and more trouble-free life than before.

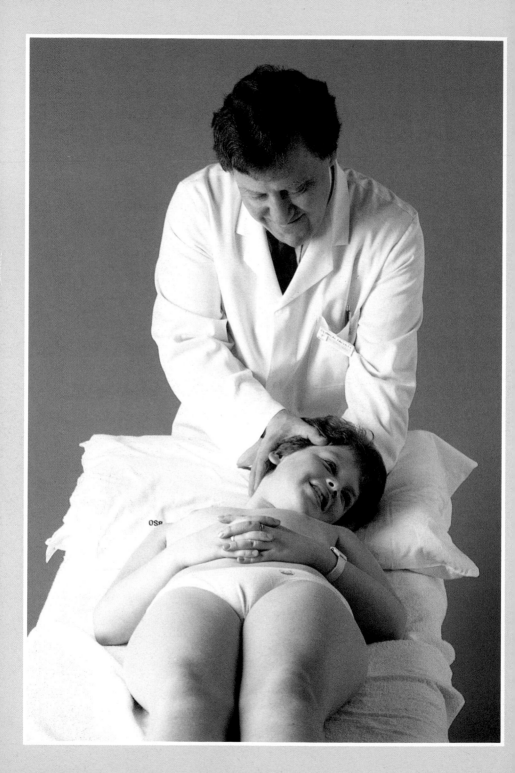

3

OSTEOPATHY
IN CONTEXT

In the United States, where osteopathy is fully recognized as a medical discipline, it is a simple matter for people who wish to enjoy the benefits of osteopathic treatment or treatment from an osteopathic viewpoint to choose a DO (doctor of osteopathy) as their medical practitioner.

In the UK and everywhere else, however, where osteopaths do not enjoy the same rights as medical practitioners, osteopathy is regarded as one of the major complementary therapies. With them, it seems to be evolving ever more rapidly into one of front-line, community-based health care. In the popular computer jargon, most alternative therapies are much more 'user-friendly' than conventional medical care. It is not surprising, therefore, that people are turning first to practitioners such as osteopaths, naturopaths, homeopaths, chiropractors and acupuncturists when they feel they have a health problem for which they would like help or advice.

Osteopathy has been trying to fulfil this role for a long time, and increasingly osteopaths are working in group practices which provide a comprehensive range of alternative health care, as well as more conventional disciplines. In the UK a single clinic may include specialists in osteopathy, naturopathy, homeopathy, acupuncture, hypnotism, herbalism, counselling, psychotherapy, chiropody, dentistry and orthodox medicine.

Osteopathy and orthodox medicine in the US and UK
In the United States there are no problems with orthodox medicine. The training of a DO is equivalent to that of an MD except that it is from an osteopathic viewpoint and includes osteopathic manipulative therapy (OMT). Therefore, in theory, your entire medical needs could be covered from a DO perspective with OMT as one of many specialisms. In the UK, osteopaths and MDs are not the same thing, but mutual contact between the two groups is increasing more frequently to the point where it becomes common for a family doctor or a hospital consultant to suggest that a patient would benefit from consulting a registered osteopath. However, the original doctor should always retain responsibility for the patient's care, and should be satisfied as to the standard of education and ethical practice of the osteopath concerned.

Not only are there regular contacts between individual doctors and osteopaths, but there are also official meetings between various bodies of doctors and osteopaths. These are

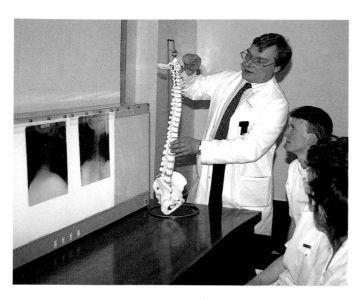

Senior students at the British School of Osteopathy in London. Anatomy, especially of the spine, forms a central part of their studies.

further strengthened by the educational contacts between the two professions, representatives of which regularly visit each other's schools, colleges and training groups. In this way confidence has built up over the years in the standards of practice and safety of registered osteopaths. So much so that, in many parts of the UK, groups of trainee doctors now have lectures from osteopaths timetabled into their programme.

Elsewhere in the world the growing recognition that osteopathy can make a valuable contribution to the care of those suffering from problems other than low back, neck or other joint pain, has brought osteopaths more into contact with other practitioners. Chiropractic is probably the nearest therapy to osteopathy, as the founder of chiropractic began his career as an osteopathy student. The differences between the therapies are discussed in Chapter 6, p. 119-122.

As well as frequent cross-referral between osteopathy and other holistic disciplines, there is also cross-referral between dentists and osteopaths, who can help greatly in the care of patients with head and neck pain arising from a poor bite, and between osteopaths and chiropodists or podiatrists caring for patients whose feet are involved in problems that manifest themselves elsewhere.

The range of patients consulting osteopaths is now so wide that it is worthwhile looking at some of these groups in detail.

Osteopathy and the treatment of children

To progress through the childhood years with as few health problems as possible is an ideal that should be pursued with great vigour. Health workers of whatever profession should take each and every opportunity that presents itself to help a child maintain (or regain) optimum health.

There is an obvious role for osteopaths to play in ensuring that the after-effects of the many minor injuries of early life are kept to a minimum. While young tissues heal quickly and well, it is important that they do so as symmetrically as possible so that mechanical stresses and strains do not proliferate.

Osteopathic treatment is ideal for children, because it is always the direct result of an examination of how that child is growing at the time. This enables the osteopath to track down the key point of sometimes complex patterns. He can then devise a management plan which takes into account the condition, the age of the child, what will happen as the child grows and, above all, *how* the child will grow. The effect of dysfunction on growing bones is of considerable importance

Children respond well to osteopathic treatment: there are few after-effects and it doesn't hurt. It can help conditions that are not obvious candidates for osteopathic treatment, such as asthma, headaches and some behaviour problems, and can also speed up convalescence after childhood illnesses.

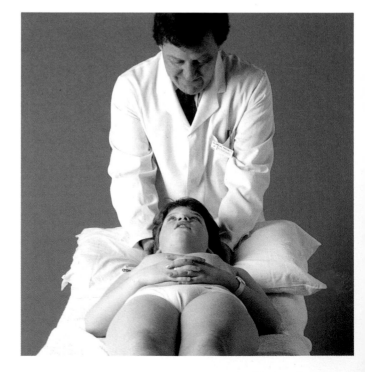

in relation to the means by which they grow, how quickly they grow, and at what age growth occurs.

The techniques used by osteopaths are also good for treating children because they are so specific and so gentle. Young patients usually find osteopathic treatment not only painless but also pleasant. Because there are no unpleasant side effects, and the child's own recuperative and restorative powers are respected as well as being reinforced, the treatment can be continued for extended periods with long intervals between treatments. This allows the osteopath to monitor the child's response to the treatments and progress, and to make subtle modifications to treatment from visit to visit.

Because osteopaths are highly skilled at using their hands to diagnose and to treat, there is little danger of them missing any serious disorder or disease, which should either be treated with different techniques or be referred to the appropriate specialist. What the patient presents with is not, therefore, always the only condition that needs treatment.

Conditions for which osteopathic treatment is helpful include many apart from obvious knocks and bumps.

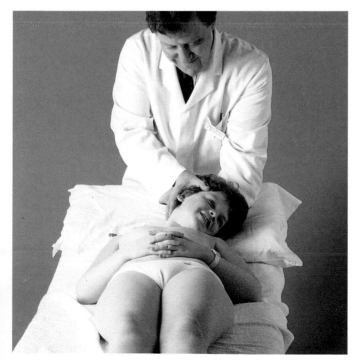

In these two pictures, the osteopath examines a child's neck and articulates it gently into rotation (that is, turns it). This is a standard procedure which is used to help diagnose the problem.

'Growing pains', asthma, headaches, foot problems, and knee pains all respond well. It is also possible to help children suffering the after-effects of such things as a traumatic birth, colic, strabismus (squint), disturbed sleep or constant crying. These conditions, all of which afflict very young children and infants particularly, are often helped by what is known as 'cranio-sacral technique' (see p. 110). This is also useful for helping children attain full recovery after common childhood illnesses such as measles, mumps, or chickenpox, and is often beneficial in minimizing the debilitating effects of the high fever that can occur during one of these diseases.

Osteopaths who practice cranio-sacral techniques have many years experience in dealing with such conditions. It is always worth consulting an osteopath about any child with a condition that is causing concern, distress and anxiety, because this treatment is often effective against all kinds of bizarre problems that cannot be 'labelled' by orthodox medicine.

Osteopathy and the elderly

The majority of health problems affecting people over sixty years of age are those to do with degeneration of one or more of their body systems. These are the conditions resulting from the wear and tear involved in a working life. A reduction in the efficiency of one part of the body has an effect on the body as a whole, because it places more demands on other organs or limbs. A good example is the way in which someone with a knee that is in an osteo-arthritic state cannot walk as well as normal. The resulting limp, although it may be mild, can consume energy two to three times faster than walking normally.

The outcome of situations such as these is an adverse drain on valuable body resources. In the later years of life tissues are slower to heal and repair. In any kind of disease, or ill-health of whatever type, the body needs to be able to devote all its attention to fighting that situation and returning to normal health.

The contribution osteopathy has to make is in lessening the impact and limiting the effect of minor mechanical and functional changes. In doing this it is possible to assist the body's own repair mechanisms not only directly – by working on the tissue or tissues affected, but also by ensuring that the peripheral stresses and strains on the body interfere as little as possible with the healing process.

Conditions for which this can be particularly effective

include osteo-arthritis of any of the joints of the arms and legs, as well as of the spine. While osteopaths do not claim to be able to repair the worn cartilage surfaces of the affected joints, by encouraging gentle stretching exercises and working on the muscles and flexibility of the joints they are frequently able to achieve a surprising amount.

By working on the muscles of the thorax, considerable relief can be obtained from the chronic respiratory problems that are often suffered in old age. Headaches and some types of dizziness or vertigo and even tinnitus are also sometimes amenable to osteopathic treatment. Far from being a form of medicine which relies on the patient being in a healthy state, osteopathy has a great deal to offer to those members of society who are no longer as fit and flexible as they once were.

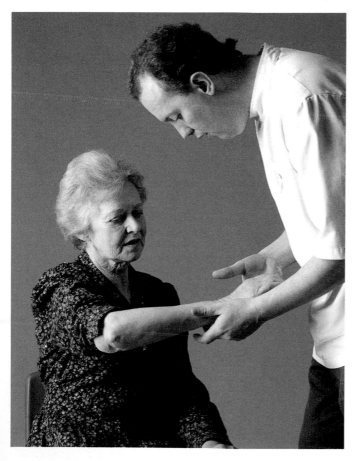

Arthritis is a debilitating condition, and osteopathy can do much to relieve the pain and to help the joints back to a useful degree of mobility.

Low-back pain is inevitable in the later stages of pregnancy, as the ligaments which support the sacro-iliac joint loosen, to allow a little mobility in the otherwise stiff joint and give the baby more room in the birth canal.

Osteopathic treatment can help relieve the pain. It can also help after the birth to get the body back into shape. It also has been known to help with milk flow problems during breastfeeding, by working directly on the malfunctioning 'let down' reflex which stimulates the flow of milk.

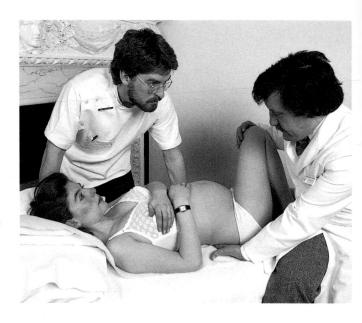

Osteopathic help during pregnancy

Many pregnant women suffering low back pain and other aches will find that an osteopath is the only person capable of looking after her in such a way that not only is her present problem relieved but also that her subsequent labour and delivery are made easier too. Osteopathy can also help with the after-effects of birth on the musculo-skeletal system. Despite this, many people are not aware that obstetrics is a field in which osteopathy can be of value.

The secret of the osteopath's success in an obstetric context is to be found in the mother's own body, which secretes a high level of a hormone called relaxin during pregnancy. This hormone has the effect of softening the ligaments – the tough fibrous structures which hold the bones together. This softening promotes the natural separation of the normally fixed pelvic bones, which occurs during the last stage of pregnancy to allow the passage of the baby's head during delivery. Most of the low back problems that osteopaths see and treat are in some way related to the way the patient carries her increased weight.

In pregnancy the average mother is going to gain up to 28 lbs (12 kg) or more. It is evident that if she has a previous history of low back pain, or if she has a postural problem that her body has up to now been able to cope with, the result of this increased weight will be enough by itself to trigger a problem and cause symptoms to occur. Add to this the fact that the structure usually responsible for holding the bones together is now naturally made weaker by the action of the hormone relaxin, and you can quickly understand why the majority of women – especially those in their late twenties or thirties – are going to suffer low back pain at some time during pregnancy.

How can an osteopath offer positive help and encouragement, and what is he going to be able to offer that normal medicine or physiotherapy is unable to provide? The answer to both of these questions lies in the registered osteopath's work and training, and the unique way that he is trained to both examine and treat his patients, pregnant or not.

The diagnostic method used involves taking a long and detailed case history of the patient, so that the full medical situation before the back pain started can be assessed. This is important because the back pain may in fact have nothing to do with the musculo-skeletal system and should therefore be investigated by a specialist in the appropriate field.

A full obstetric history is also essential, including the number and outcome of previous pregnancies. Did the woman deliver her previous children naturally, or was a Caesarian section necessary? Is there a history of miscarriage and, if so, at what stage in the pregnancy? It should be emphasized at this juncture that osteopathic treatment cannot cause a miscarriage unless the osteopath is foolish enough to be treating a patient who has a history of miscarriage, using extremely violent techniques, very early in the pregnancy. There is no such thing as an 'osteopathic abortion'! However, it is statistically recognized that if a woman is going to abort, then the commonest time for this to happen is at the time of the expected third and fourth missed periods. Most osteopaths would not treat a patient at this time, although this does not imply that osteopathic treatment is in any way dangerous. Osteopaths believe that *any* extreme physical activity at this time is probably best avoided.

After taking the case history, the osteopath allows plenty of time to examine the patient. He is interested both in her posture and in the way that her body is coping with the extra demands to which it is being subjected. In fact a woman's posture will change radically three times during the course of her pregnancy as the pelvis tilts and the muscles contract and tighten.

The osteopath will also want to look for such things as spinal curvatures and previous fractures, since any of these will affect the way that the body adapts to the changing strain imposed by the expanding uterus. Next his examination will assess the tissues under stress to try to determine the mobility and quality of the movement.

In treating the patient, gentle techniques are used to relax the muscular tissues. If a muscle is tight and fibrotic, or 'gristly', it cannot relax. If it cannot relax it soon fatigues and thus is unable to function as it should.

Likewise the ligaments are being stretched in preparation for the impending delivery. Osteopathic treatment stretches them only to the limit of safety. This means that when the time comes for the bones of the pelvis to separate to allow the baby's head to pass, the separation will happen more easily, making labour shorter and more comfortable than it would otherwise have been.

In addition many of the other misfortunes associated with pregnancy can be helped by osteopathic treatment. The stresses and strains which produce indigestion, haemorrhoids, tingling in the fingers, aching feet and ankles and other niggling problems can often be greatly smoothed by osteopathic treatment. It can also be a valuable aid to other pre-natal classes and exercises.

The real difference between osteopathic treatment and any other form of treatment during pregnancy is that at this time, more than any other, the detailed analysis of the patient's posture is vital. Many other professionals, such as midwives and obstetricians, are not trained to do this. It is also vital for it to be done at the right time if the body is to be helped to overcome its pain.

Osteopathy and sport

As more and more people participate in sports at all levels, injuries related to 'athletic trauma' are becoming far more common. All too often medical practitioners take the attitude that if patients are silly enough to take the risk and put themselves in a position where they can be injured, then they deserve to suffer. Amateurs who are keen to return to competition, training, or just running for the fun of it can have considerable trouble getting the right sort of skilled help and advice that they need. They certainly often fail to get the encouragement they deserve for taking the trouble to get fitter and healthier, and looking after themselves in general.

The lithe shapes of professional basketball players in action seem to curve through the air with effortless ease to the spectator; but the players pay for such elegant exertions with strained ligaments and torn muscles. Increasingly osteopathy is being taken up by sports players both to treat injury and as a preventive therapy.

Sporting injuries Typical injuries that osteopaths commonly treat
● Tennis elbow
● Golfer's elbow
● Biceps tendonitis
● Hyperextension strains in divers or swimmers
● Pushed elbow joints and wrist joints in martial artists
● Spondylolisthesis in judo exponents
● Low back injuries in weightlifters
● Shin splints and foot arch problems in marathon runners
● Groin strains and sacro-iliac injuries in footballers
● Postural problems in dressage riders and show jumpers
● Hip joint problems in dancers

The osteopathic approach to dealing with patients is well suited to helping athletes of all standards, whatever their sport. By virtue of his training in analysing the mechanical components of all sorts of diseases, and all sorts of complex movements, the osteopath is able to critically evaluate not only the athlete's problem but also its origins and precisely what relation it has to the sport. These may be linked either to the physical aspects of training or playing, or to the psychological aspects of the athlete's motivation and physical/mental state while performing either against another competitor or team, or against the clock and past achievements.

Giving an athlete full and comprehensive osteopathic care involves not only helping his or her symptomatic state, but also helping in the analysis of how he or she is going about playing the sport. The osteopath who specializes in sports medicine will undertake a thorough investigation of the athlete's equipment, training schedules and technique, as well as his or her physical state and fitness; he will also explore the athlete's attitude. This can be especially important when the athlete is committed to participating in a heavy schedule of fixtures. It is not unknown for sportsmen and women to take greater risks of injury on the (unconscious) grounds that being injured is the only really valid excuse for not playing.

It is becoming increasingly common for sports clubs and teams of all sizes and levels, in many different sports, to have strong official links with a particular osteopath. Examples of this include international volleyball and judo squads, rugby and hockey clubs, and American football at both league and club level. Many international sportsmen such as tennis and cricket players, runners, swimmers, cyclists, and rally and racing drivers all consult osteopaths.

It is also becoming a familiar sight to see an osteopath actually at a sporting venue giving immediate treatment and advice to athletes during the course of an event. In the recent past, osteopaths have adopted travelling advisory roles to rally teams, volleyball, hockey, and gridiron football teams, and to individual tennis players and golfers.

By their involvement in sports in all ways, osteopaths are contributing in a major way to the capacity of the individuals concerned to live life to the full in the way that they want to live it. They are also making a major effort to allow society to function as fully and completely as possible in an area that is essential if its members are to get an adequate feeling of freedom and fellowship in balancing work with play.

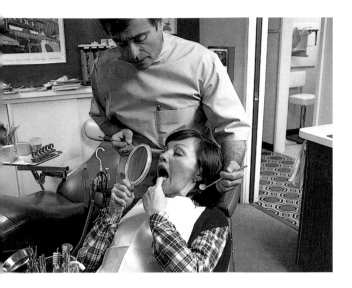

Dentistry and osteopathy don't spring to mind as likely partners, but osteopathy can be very effective after orthodontic treatment which changes the 'bite'. A new bite will put completely new strains on the muscles and joints of the face and jaw, and osteopathy can help patients deal with that without recourse to pain killers.

Osteopathy and the dentist

At first sight the link between dental conditions and osteopathic treatment might seem obscure. However, it is becoming increasingly accepted by the dental profession that the efficiency of a patient's 'bite' is closely linked with the posture and movement of the head and neck, in particular, but also of the rest of the body as well.

This is because the tiny sensors in the temporo-mandibular joint – the joint between the lower jaw and the skull – influence the way the head and neck are held. In addition, orthodontic work to modify the alignment of the teeth and how they meet in the bite is made more effective when backed up by osteopathic cranio-sacral techniques (see pp. 110-1). This can make it much easier for the bones of the skull to adapt to the new shape that is being asked of them. Other types of osteopathic treatment can also be effective in helping the muscles of the jaws, face and the rest of the head and neck to compensate for any changes demanded by dental work.

Osteopaths also see patients who are suffering pain as a result of arthritis in the temporo-mandibular joint. This is a very painful condition that can lead to pain in the face, jaw and neck, headaches and tinnitus. Direct treatment to the joints, the muscles around them, and to the upper part of the neck can be effective in minimizing the discomfort felt in these cases even before the osteopath decides it may be necessary to refer the patient to a dental specialist.

Osteopathy and the disabled

The physically and mentally handicapped are a section of the community with whom, at first glance, there would seem to be no obvious role for an osteopath. However, many disabled people have tremendous difficulty using their bodies as they would wish or are potentially able to do. Consequently they frequently suffer chronic musculo-skeletal aches and pains which they are not always able to communicate.

For example, someone who is confined to life in a wheelchair has to perform every task using the muscles of the trunk and shoulder girdle. Loss of the capacity to use the muscles of the pelvis and legs, as well as the loss of the participation of those parts of the body in a stabilizing and counterbalancing role, totally changes the pattern of muscle development, of joint stress, and of wear and tear.

The same is true of someone who always has to use a walking-stick or crutches, or a walking frame. The after-effects of amputations or other less drastic surgical procedures can leave the patient at a severe mechanical disadvantage which leads to the accumulation of stress and strain over many years. Those who suffer even mild forms of blindness and deafness

Wheelchair athletes in a desperate race to the finish in the LA Wheelchair Olympics. The enormous strain that these athletes put the top part of the body under can be relieved by osteopathic treatment and specially designed exercises.

also tend, over a period of years, to adopt a particular posture, which may distort the normal balance of muscles or bones. Again, it is fairly common that an osteopath can provide considerable relief for patients suffering from any of these conditions.

Patients suffering some form of mental disability, often have diminished capacity for co-ordination and motor control. This places a strain on their muscles and joints. The reason for this may be because they have to spend a lot of their time in a special chair or bed in a restricted position, or because they have to adopt a contorted posture in order to move or even to remain upright. Patients with these handicaps often benefit from osteopathic treatment that can give them a tiny bit more control and can hopefully also improve their physical co-ordination.

Others who may benefit from osteopathic treatment include children who have suffered some form of birth trauma, as well as children with Down's syndrome. Osteopaths do not claim to be able to reverse irreversible states. What they do find, however, is that their form of treatment can make small changes that provide the patient with a significant improvement in the quality of his or her life. Where the patient concerned is still learning and growing, this is vitally important.

Osteopathy and the future

Osteopathy, while remaining true to its fundamental principles, has to re-examine its methods and ideas constantly in order to survive. The simple fact of committing as much time and effort as possible to provide an education that is both comprehensive and challenging ensures that osteopathic philosophy will develop. By being unwilling to simply repeat the same formula year after year, osteopaths can gradually clarify, modify and extend the scope and application of osteopathic treatment.

In the United States as has been said, osteopaths enjoy greater freedom than their counterparts in other countries, so interdisciplinary liaison is unfettered. In the UK and Europe, osteopathy has made overtures.

The equipping, staffing and improvement of centres of education, capable of holding a realistic and meaningful scientific dialogue with other educational establishments of the highest quality, such as universities, polytechnics and medical schools, means that students and staff mix with and are exposed to leaders in other related fields.

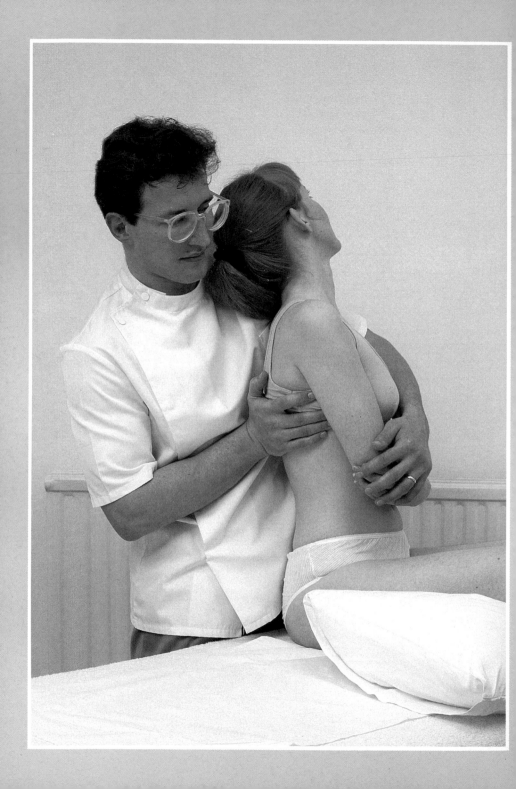

4

HOW
OSTEOPATHY
WORKS

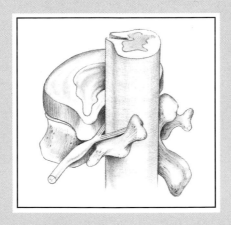

How does osteopathy work? How can osteopathic manipulation have often dramatic effects, offering relief and help to people whose own family doctor can give them nothing but painkillers and instructions to lie down until the pain goes away?

The theory behind osteopathy is simple – more straightforward to the Western mind than other complementary therapies such as acupuncture, which depends on a grasp of Eastern philosophical concepts. There is no mystery surrounding osteopathy. To understand how it works, you need to understand the theory propounded by Dr Andrew Taylor Still and to have some elementary knowledge of how the human body works.

The basic tenet of osteopathy is that structure governs function. That is, if bodily structures are damaged or deformed, their function is impaired. Osteopathy works by finding out in what way the structure is damaged, and adjusting or modifying it so that the damage is repaired or minimized. Alteration or modification is achieved by working on muscles, bones and nerves, which function together as the neuro-musculo-skeletal (NMS) system. In the osteopath's view, the NMS system is the key to the rest of the body. Osteopaths work directly on this body system, either to solve problems in the system itself or to create the optimum environment for the other organs to function properly.

To understand osteopathic theory in practice requires an understanding of how the neuro-musculo-skeletal system works.

The neuro-musculo-skeletal system (NMS)

Every breath we take, every movement we make, every expression, action or emotion is relayed to the world using the neuro-musculo-skeletal system. From facial expression to speech, from making money to making mayhem, all action requires the co-ordinated function of nerves, muscles and bones. Anything we do in life and any response we might make on the conscious or unconscious levels is mediated by the NMS.

Dr Still placed great emphasis on the NMS, regarding it not only as a protector of vital organs, but also as the prime organizer of normal, healthy life. Professor Irwin Korr, in the 1967 Scott Memorial Lecture to the American Academy of Osteopathy, put it this way:

*Human activity is the continuing changing composite of the
activities of striated muscles, most of them pulling on bony levers,
their contractions and relaxations orchestrated by the central nervous
system in response to external and internal stimuli and to volition.*

Although the NMS is a system of interrelating, interdependent sub-systems, understanding how it works entails a brief survey of each of its three parts: muscles, bones and nerves.

If you look in the index of any standard medical textbook of human anatomy, you will find named 212 bones, 145 muscles – all paired except for the diaphragm – and 119 nerves. Muscles cannot act without the stimulation provided by the nervous system or without the anchoring skeletal system to pull on. The nervous system has to be supported by the skeletal system for its own safety and protection, which is why the brain and the spinal cord are housed inside the bony skull and vertebral column.

The skeletal system needs regular movement if it is not to lose minerals (especially calcium) and become brittle. This is why physiotherapists visit patients who are confined to bed for long periods of time, to give them exercises and so prevent the development of osteoporosis (brittle bones).

Muscles, bones and internal organs are controlled by the nervous system. There are two parts to the human nervous system: the central system (CNS) and the autonomic nervous system (ANS). The central nervous system is directed from the brain and its extension, the spinal cord. The autonomic nervous system, which also uses the spinal cord as its command post, appears to be independent of the brain. In either system, the function of nerves is to relay information and instruction in a continuous, self-modifying flow.

Messages are transmitted along nerves in the form of tiny electrical impulses. These travel from the brain and spinal cord to the organ concerned and modify its function. The central nervous system governs voluntary movement, which is brought about by the action of the motor nerves which run to the muscles. Information is fed back into the CNS from the muscles concerned so that the movements are co-ordinated. The autonomic nervous system governs involuntary movements such as digestion, pupil dilation, and breathing.

The CNS is kept aware of the outside world by the senses of sight, smell, hearing and taste and via sense organs such as those in the skin which respond to touch, pain, temperature and the proximity of objects or obstacles. This information, together with that from the muscles, travels along special sensory nerves back to the central nervous system.

The analogy of a home heating system may help to clarify how the central nervous system works. If the temperature drops below a certain level, the thermostat senses the cold and passes the information on to the switching mechanism, which starts the boiler. This then heats the water and the pump moves it around the radiators in each room of the house. These warm the rooms, and when the temperature rises above the level set on the thermostat, it senses this, and shuts the system down. This system is automatic and it relies on a number of factors in order to function properly. First, there must be a means of sensing change in temperature. Second, there must be a way of transmitting that information to a control point. Third, there must be a means whereby the control point effects the necessary change and last, a means whereby that change is monitored by the sensors.

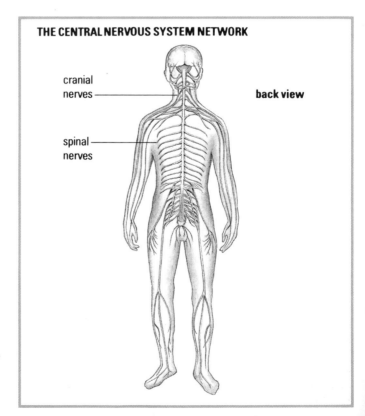

THE CENTRAL NERVOUS SYSTEM NETWORK

cranial nerves

back view

spinal nerves

The central nervous system consists of the brain and spinal cord, with nerves extending from the spinal cord to the periphery of body. These govern sensory and motor activities.

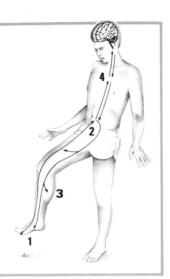

THE REFLEX ARC IN ACTION
*No-one stops to think when they
unwittingly step on a drawing
pin (1). The body takes over,
jerking the foot away by reflex
action. The message from nerves
in the foot is processed in the
spine. (2). From this command
centre, one message is passed
directly back to the foot ordering
it to move (3). At the same time,
a message is relayed to the brain,
informing it of what has
happened so that it can direct
further action if necessary (4).*

The reflex arcs

The human body has a number of automatic pathways just
like the central heating system. They are there to act as a
defence. These pathways are called reflex arcs, because they
produce a reaction extremely fast and are independent of the
brain's control.

A good example of a reflex arc (or reflex pathway, as they
are sometimes called), is what happens when a person steps on
a tack. Before the brain registers the fact that the foot is in pain,
the body's defence mechanisms have swung into action to
protect it from further damage, by causing the muscles to
contract and thus draw the foot up and away from the tack, all
in milliseconds. When a physician taps the knee with a patella
hammer, he makes use of this type of reflex to check that the
nervous system is functioning properly. This is the well-
known knee-jerk reflex.

The reflex pathway is very important in osteopathy. This is
the point at which the osteopath can intervene to change or
modify the messages relayed around the central nervous
system. Because these reflexes bypass the brain, there is no
conscious interference from the patient. The osteopath can
manipulate or treat the muscle or joint, using various
techniques. Following treatment, the nerves transmit slightly
different information back to base, receiving in turn different
instructions. Under the close control of the osteopath, the
modification process is underway.

Osteopathic treatment

How is the theory of structural modification put into practice by the osteopath? And how can the general principles of osteopathy relate to the particular needs of the individual patient?

Osteopathic treatment is different for every patient and for every case. It is even different for each individual patient at each consultation. Questions such as 'What do osteopaths do for sports injuries?' or 'How does the osteopath treat a slipped disc?' are very difficult to answer, because each case is different according to the specific factors that initiated tissue break-down at that particular time.

However, in all cases, at whatever stage, the aim of the osteopath is to effect change in the neuro-musculo-skeletal system. This change is brought about by an osteopathic technique, chosen after careful diagnosis. Each treatment consists of many different techniques selected for differing reasons.

Soft tissue treatment and the muscular system

One very common technique that almost all osteopaths use is called Soft Tissue Treatment. To the patient, a general massage to relax tired muscle and a soft tissue treatment may be indistinguishable, but to the trained hand of the therapist, it is not the same thing at all.

Massage is non-specific and aimed at whole regions of the body or even at the whole body. It may be stimulating or relaxing, but generally the aim is to loosen tight tissue and improve the circulation to a particular region.

Osteopathic soft tissue treatment, on the other hand, is always performed with a definite aim in mind. 'Find it, fix it and leave it alone' is a famous osteopathic aphorism, taught wherever osteopathic students learn their techniques. The trained osteopath is feeling all the time for the responses of the tissue to his treating hand, whether it be relaxation or stimulation of the muscle under his or her fingers. This 'palpatory awareness', as it is called, is central to all good technique. If the muscle responds quickly, then the osteopath stops and moves on. Soft tissue treatment is very different from massage in that it is not time-orientated. It is not a question of a statutory ten minutes of treatment and then the osteopath stops; the treatment comes to an end when it has effected a change in the tissue. There are many forms of massage machines, with and without timers, but none of these

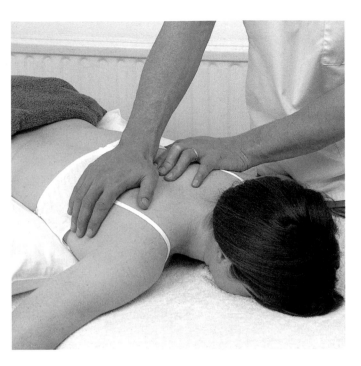

*Soft tissue treatment to the
shoulder region. The aim
is to relax high muscle
tension and restore
mobility.*

*Soft tissue treatment
applied in a slightly
different position. Soft
tissue treatment is used for
as long as it takes for the
muscle to respond and for
the osteopath to detect the
change. It should never be
confused with massage,
which goes on for a fixed
amount of time regardless
of any change in the
patient.*

There are three kinds of muscle in the body: skeletal, or striated which moves the body about; involuntary, or smooth, which governs the function of the gut and other organs; and cardiac, which drives the heart. Most of our muscles are skeletal, and work by contraction. Each muscle is made up of a bundle of muscle fibres, which is in turn made up from bundles of myofibrils. Each myofibril contains strands of the proteins actin and myosin, bound together in a membrane sheath. The proteins respond to nervous stimulus by contracting in concert, making movement possible.

have the ability to perceive the tissues' response. For this reason, there could never be an osteopathic machine. You might find some osteopaths who use massage machines in their practice, but this is the exception rather than the rule.

How does soft tissue treatment ease pain? What happens to the muscle when the osteopath begins to work on it? How does the muscle relax or tighten up, and why? There are a number of differing theories on these points. The two most credible of these theories are the theory of fluid exchange and the theory of reflex relaxation.

Fluid exchange

One way that the body lets us know that all is not well on a cellular level is with pain. When the blood flow to the tissue is impaired, the tissue becomes painful. The greater the rate of metabolism (the chemical breakdown of nutrients) within the tissue, the more rapid the onset of pain. It is known as ischaemic pain. Ischaemia is the insufficient supply of blood to any part of the body.

As a muscle contracts, it compresses thousands of tiny blood vessels and so cuts off its own blood supply and drainage. Fluid exchange is thus impaired. The muscular contraction increases the rate of metabolism within the tissue and thus produces more waste material, such as lactic acid, the accumulation of

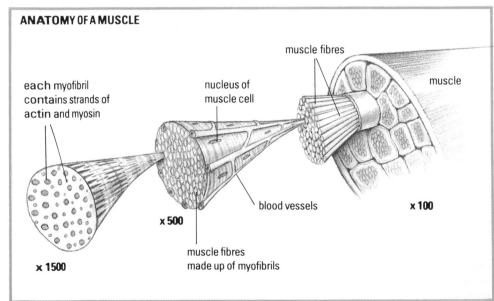

ANATOMY OF A MUSCLE

each myofibril contains strands of actin and myosin

nucleus of muscle cell

muscle fibres

muscle

blood vessels

x 100

x 500

x 1500

muscle fibres made up of myofibrils

which is painful. This is what can happen to athletes, particularly runners. The exact cause of ischaemic pain is unknown, but it can be relieved by supplying oxygen to the tissues locally.

The theory is that soft tissue treatment works by relaxing contracted muscles to re-establish the flow of blood through the veins, and by speeding up the elimination of waste products. Muscle is made up of thousands of fibres bound together in bundles. These bundles in turn are bound up into collections of bigger bundles and so on exactly in the same way that rope is made. As the muscle is massaged, so the fluid that has collected as a result of the contraction is pushed out of the muscle in the spaces between the fibres. This leaves room for fresh blood loaded with oxygen and other nutrients to penetrate to the tissues, relieving the pain and stiffness.

Reflex relaxation

The theory of reflex relaxation holds that pain can be relieved by intervening to change the shape or tone of a muscle. Soft tissue treatment can modify the information transmitted along the reflex pathway or to the brain. In response, different instructions come back, altering the way the muscle behaves.

There are many different nerve endings in a muscle, each with a specific function. Some are receptive to stretching along the length of the muscle and some to stretching across it. Some are receptive to compression and others to twisting movements. Much of the information going to and from the muscle is transmitted along the reflex arcs mentioned earlier. As the osteopath works on the muscle either to stimulate it or to stretch it, he or she works via these reflex arcs and the muscle spindles and tendon organs (the names given to the nerve receptors in muscles and tendons). The osteopath is able to influence the length and tone of the muscles so that they are better able to move or relax as the tissues demand.

Touch as therapy

The subject of soft tissue treatment cannot be left without recognizing the psychological interplay between the therapist and the patient that centres around physical touch.

Touching is vital to normal human function and emotion. We need to touch and be touched in return. If we are forced to exist in a world deprived of tactile stimulation, we soon become disorientated and part company with reality. The same thing happens if we are over-stimulated. Sophisticated

REFLEX ARC IN THE AUTONOMIC NERVOUS SYSTEM

spinal cord

A reflex arc in the autonomic nervous system shows how a nerve stimulus prompts the sympathetic nerves into action to stimulate muscular activity. The stimulus travels from the receptor in skin, muscle etc (1) along a nerve to the spinal cord (2). A connecting nerve in the spinal cord relays the information (3) and the impulse is carried from the spinal cord along another nerve (4) through connecting stations outside (5) to smooth muscle, skin, skeletal muscle, sweat glands (6).

torture and interrogation techniques unfortunately use these facts all too often. Western medicine has allowed itself to become less and less of a touching profession. The orthodox doctor often diagnoses by case history, X-ray and laboratory testing, using only minimal palpation. He or she treats by and large with the spoken word, the drug company or the knife, all undeniably powerful in their own way, but are they enough? To deny touch as a therapeutic tool is to deny something as old as healing itself, and modern Western medicine is in grave danger of becoming a hands-off profession.

When a child falls over and bangs his knee, his mother rubs it better. If we as adults bang our knee, the first impulse is to rub it and support it. Neither we, nor our mothers, nor their mothers before them may have understood the biochemistry of that action. Rubbing stimulates the release of powerful painkilling chemicals, called endorphins, at the damage site. All the human animal knows is that rubbing eases the pain.

In modern therapeutics, where is the therapist who rubs pain away? One of the reasons behind the success of massage as a therapy is its appeal to this very basic instinct. Massage feels good and takes away general aches, pains and weariness. Osteopathic soft tissue treatment feels good as well as being very effective in treating muscle pain.

Osteopathic treatment and joints

One of the things that osteopathy has become famous for over the years has been the manipulation of joints. This is known by the layman as joint cracking or popping and by the orthodox medical profession as manipulation. To osteopaths it is known as a High Velocity Thrust (HVT). Once again, there are many theories that try to explain why it works.

One fact, now universally accepted, is that the crack of a manipulation has nothing to do with bones going in or out of place. A bone that is out of position is dislocated, and dislocations are the province of the orthopaedic surgeon. (In the USA, there are DOs who specialize in orthopaedic surgery.)

In most cases, wherever bones meet, they form a flexible joint (called a synovial joint). Synovial joints are enclosed in a tough, fibrous capsule which is lined with a thin secretory lining known as the synovial membrane. This membrane secretes synovial fluid which lubricates the joint. Within the capsule, the joint surfaces are held together by a partial vacuum, in other words, the pressure inside the joint capsule is

A SYNOVIAL JOINT

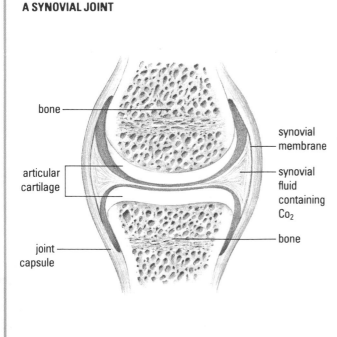

bone

articular cartilage

joint capsule

synovial membrane

synovial fluid containing CO_2

bone

Wherever bones come together in the body, they are encased in a synovial joint. (Exceptions are the bones of the pelvis and the bones of the skull.) The ends of each bone are coated in smooth cartilage so that they do not grate together. The tough fibrous capsule that wraps around them is lined with synovial membrane, which secretes synovial fluid. This lubricates the bones so that they can move together without friction.

slightly less than the surrounding atmospheric pressure. When a joint is manipulated, the joint surfaces are separated slightly. This disturbs the normal pressure in the capsule, allowing millions of tiny bubbles of gas (carbon dioxide) to come out of solution. It is exactly the same principle with a bottle of fizzy drink. If you shake the bottle but do not release the cap, nothing happens, but if you loosen the cap and equalize the pressures inside and outside of the bottle, the drink fizzes as bubbles come out of solution.

It is this release of gas that causes the popping sound. This explains why joints cannot be 'cracked' twice in quick succession. It takes time for the bubbles of gas to dissolve into the synovial fluid again.

How can 'popping' the joints help to relieve muscle pain? It is not the release of the gas itself, but the effect of stretching the joint capsule that the osteopath is aiming at.

We come back once again to the reflex arc. The diagram

A SPINAL REFLEX

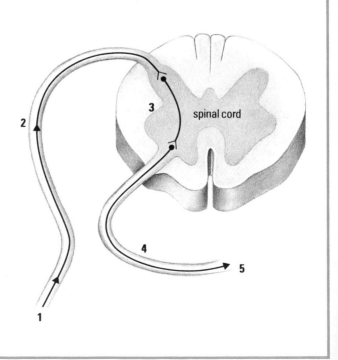

This spinal reflex shows how osteopathic work on a joint can influence muscle activity.

Stimulus from joint capsule (1) travels along a nerve to spinal cord (2) through a connecting nerve in the spinal cord (3) and out along another nerve (4) to skeletal muscle which responds to the stimulus (5).

shows that nerves link the joint capsule and the surrounding muscle via a reflex arc involving the spinal cord at the level concerned. As the osteopath manipulates the joint, nerves in the capsule send a modified impulse along the nerve pathway and back again. In response, the muscle surrounding the joint relaxes and lets go. It is as simple as that.

It is this that is responsible for the diminution of muscle spasm and the increased range of movement which people experience – sometimes it seems miraculously – after HVT treatment.

A manipulation takes a couple of seconds, while a complete osteopathic treatment takes up to half an hour. Therefore, it should be obvious that a manipulation of this nature forms only a small part of an osteopathic treatment, and it is only one of a number of tools in the osteopathic toolbox that is used during a treatment if the patient needs it. The terms osteopathy and manipulation are not, therefore, synonymous.

The classic osteopathic technique is the High Velocity Thrust to the thoracic spine (rib area). It is known irreverently as 'the dog', after an incident in an apocryphal tale of an osteopathic convention in Chicago. When this technique was being demonstrated, a voice was heard to call from the assembled practitioners, 'I wouldn't do that to my dog!' Whatever the canine connection, it is still an effective technique.

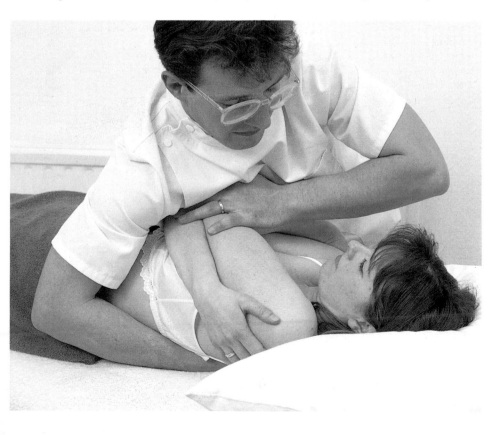

Passive movement techniques and articulation

Passive movement means movement made by (or more accurately, to) the patient's body without the active involvement of the patient. That is, the osteopath moves the patient's limbs, and all the patient has to do is let it happen. This technique, coupled with palpation, helps the osteopath to diagnose a problem. Passive movement techniques are used together with HVT and soft tissue treatment, or on their own.

Articulation is a passive movement technique. Osteopathic articulation does not involve the fearsome rack-like machinery seen in some physiotherapy departments. It means a gentle stretching of the tissues, sometimes with the use of levers. These 'levers' are usually the patient's own arms and legs. Levering makes the treatment less painful for the patient as it minimizes the amount of pressure required. Manual traction involves the osteopath gently stretching the whole trunk. Like soft tissue treatment, passive movement techniques are constantly monitored by the osteopath's palpating hands, searching for tissue response.

Passive articulation of the spine while the patient is sitting. Passive articulation can be both a diagnostic tool and a treatment in itself.

The osteopath articulates a joint (that is, takes through its normal range of movement), while the patient makes no contribution other than sitting still and letting it happen. It is a very useful way of checking on the progress of a course of treatment. As the joint becomes more mobile, so articulation should become easier.

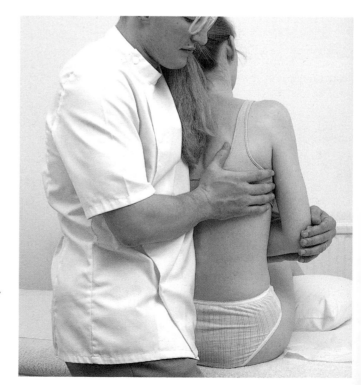

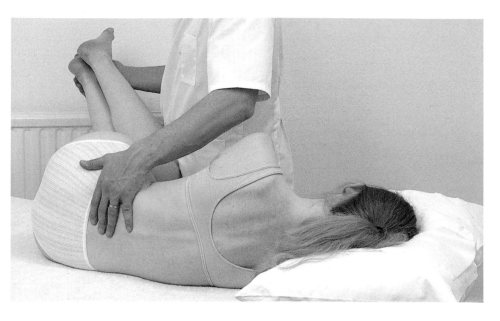

The neuro-musculo-skeletal system and the organs

How does the neuro-musculo-skeletal system influence organ function? Before this question may be answered, it is necessary to discuss the second branch of the body's nervous system, the autonomic nervous system (ANS).

This is the automatic part of the nervous system that controls the heart, the secretory glands and involuntary muscle. Involuntary muscle is muscle that is not under conscious control: for example, muscles in the walls of the bladder and the bowels, the pupil of the eye, and muscles in the walls of blood vessels.

The control system for this involuntary muscle operates in two parts: the sympathetic and the parasympathetic nervous systems. The two systems are separate, but work closely with one another. For example, the parasympathetic system causes the gut to contract, and the sympathetic system makes it relax; these two movements combine to move food along the gut.

Anatomically, these two nervous systems originate in totally different places. The parasympathetic system originates in the head and 'tail' region of the spine, and thus is known as the cranio-sacral system. The sympathetic system, on the other hand, originates in the middle or 'thoracic' area of the spine.

Once again, we meet a complex group of reflexes built into this set-up, built into the spinal cord and the autonomic

Passive articulation of the lumbar spine, while the patient is lying down. Once again, this technique can be used either as a diagnostic aid (to assess flexibility and degree of mobility) or a treatment. In diagnosis, the osteopath will try passive articulation from all different angles – from the front, the side, with the patient sitting, standing or lying – all the time refining and affirming his original assessment.

THE AUTONOMIC NERVOUS SYSTEM

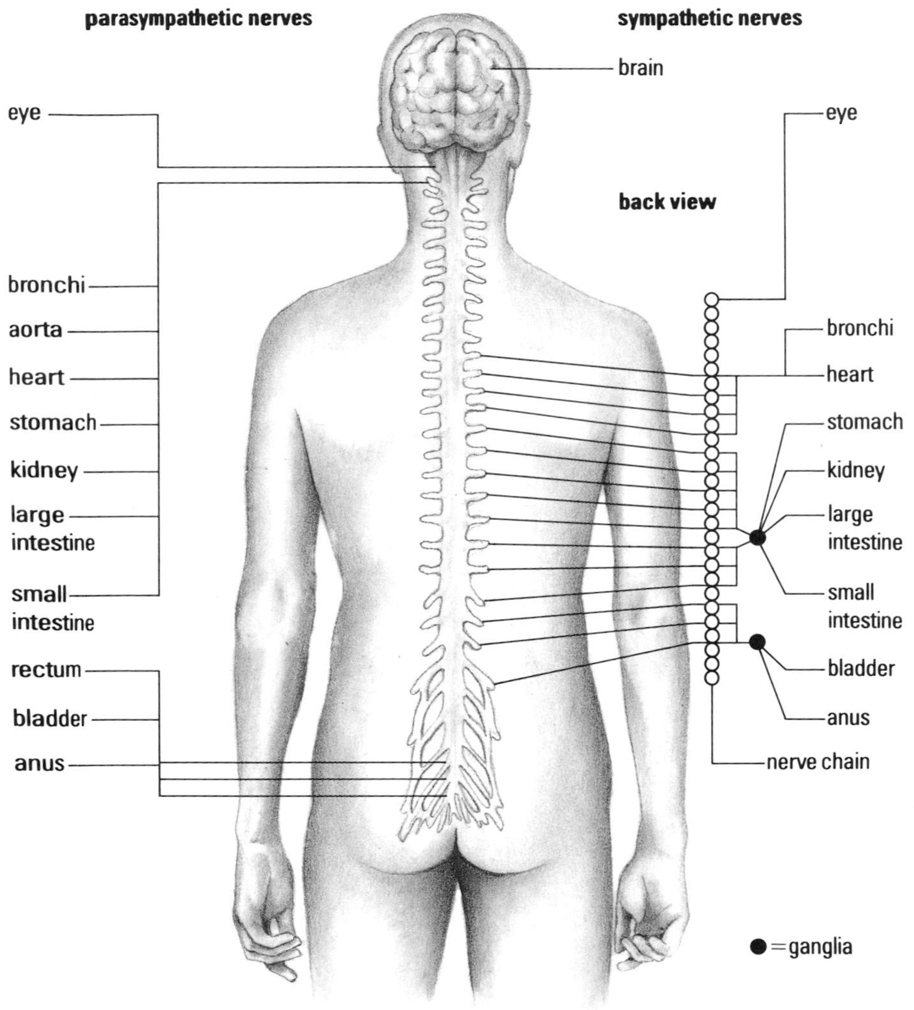

parasympathetic nerves   **sympathetic nerves**

brain

eye

back view

eye

bronchi
aorta
heart
stomach
kidney
large
intestine
small
intestine
rectum
bladder
anus

bronchi
heart
stomach
kidney
large
intestine
small
intestine
bladder
anus
nerve chain

● =ganglia

A stylized view of the two halves of the autonomous nervous system which work in harmony. The sympathetic nerves influence muscle activity, first passing from the spine to a central nerve chain. They dominate the partnership when rapid or strenuous action is called for. The parasympathetic nerves, which pass directly from the spine to the muscles and organs they control, decrease muscular activity. They are the dominant partner when the body is at rest.

nervous system. This time, however, the reflexes have a number of different possible alternative connections. They can run from one organ to another via the spinal cord, or from an organ to the skin or spinal muscles, or even from the skin and spinal muscles back to the organs. They also connect up within the spinal cord with nerve pathways running up and down the cord and so connect with the brain.

Much research work has been done in the USA at the Department of Osteopathy at Michigan State University on these reflex pathways, principally by Professor William Johnson. He has used thermographic film to demonstrate the presence of 'hot spots' in the skin of the back of patients who have had heart attacks. The results clearly show that the hotter these zones are, the more recent the acute lesions. Also, if there are chronic problems with angina or ischaemic changes in the heart muscle, the regions become darker.

Professor Johnson and his team have worked both in the laboratory and in clinics, to try to influence diseased organs by manipulating the spine and surrounding soft tissues in an attempt to interrupt and change these reflex pathways. One study showed that patients who had been treated using osteopathic manipulative therapy while in the intensive care unit, recovered more quickly than those in the control group. These experiments are even now being repeated and revalidated, but the connections between the autonomic nervous system and the neuro–musculo–skeletal system is real and available, thus opening up wide areas of treatment possibilities for osteopaths to use.

The disc myth About 44% of osteopathic patients worldwide present to the osteopath with back pain. A high proportion believe that they have a 'slipped disc', because this is still a common medical diagnosis when the patient presents to the family doctor with an acute back attack.

Discs do not slip. They are held in place very firmly indeed with some of the strongest ligaments that the body possesses. Instead, they can dry out and then crack open, allowing the soft jelly centre to be squeezed out under gravity and come to press against the nearby nerve, causing excrutiating pain often in a leg. Back sufferers think that something has slipped out because it feels as if something is actually out of place.

Osteopathic treatment and disc injuries

Large numbers of people who seek relief in the osteopath's hands shuffle and occasionally crawl into the consulting room complaining of back pain. Most of them think that there is something wrong with one of their intervertebral discs. These discs are pads of fatty tissue that separate the bony vertebrae. They receive more blame for acute back pain than any other tissue in the body, and for the most part, this blame is misplaced. The slipped or ruptured disc is not the main cause of back pain at all. Most disc-associated back pain is caused by ligament damage and muscle spasm. The osteopath can help relieve this kind of pain. Osteopaths, however, cannot 'put the disc back'. Nobody can. The patient who comes in and is miraculously put right in one treatment is, in effect, not suffering from an acute prolapsed disc at all.

THE SPINE AND ITS LIGAMENTS

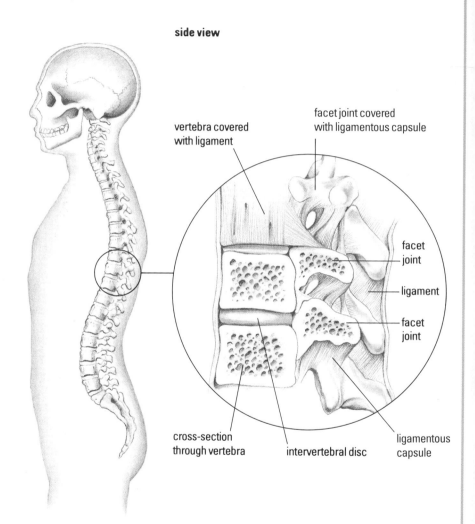

side view

vertebra covered with ligament

facet joint covered with ligamentous capsule

facet joint

ligament

facet joint

cross-section through vertebra

intervertebral disc

ligamentous capsule

The joints of the spine are bound together by a system of tough ligaments which extend right around the spinal column.

Understanding your back

To understand how osteopathy can help back pain, you have to understand how your back works. The backbone is made up of a column of bony vertebrae sandwiched together with intervertebral discs. A typical intervertebral disc looks a little like an onion with a soft jelly centre. The layers on the outside of the disc are called the annulus, and the soft jelly centre is called the nucleus. The disc is firmly bound to the bones above and below and to two thick, gristly ligaments to the front and behind. These ligaments pass right down the spine from the top of the neck to the base, and they bind the whole thing firmly together, bones, discs and all, in one long moving chain. They are known as the anterior and posterior longitudinal ligaments and they have many pain-sensitive nerve endings attached to them, especially close to the disc. That is why such agony is experienced when these ligaments are overstretched or pulled sharply.

A thing of beauty is a joy forever, but not if it starts to hurt! Too many of us neglect the way we sit or stand and adopt a slouching posture which can become habitual and cause all sorts of trouble later on. By all means laze on a sunny beach, but take care of your back as well as your suntan.

DISC PROTRUSION AND NERVE PAIN

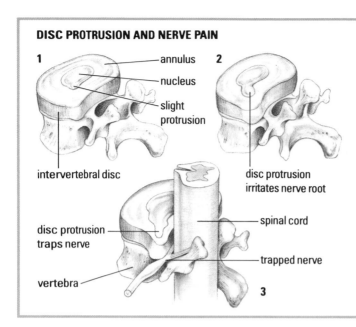

1 annulus
nucleus
slight
protrusion
intervertebral disc

2 disc protrusion
irritates nerve root

disc protrusion
traps nerve

spinal cord

vertebra

trapped nerve

3

If the annulus of a spinal disc ruptures, it forces the nucleus out of its inter-vertebral position. This can lead to discomfort and pain in various degrees, depending on how far the disc protrudes.

Slight protrusion will lead to referred pain in the hip and thigh (1); a larger bulge will irritate the nerve root, causing sciatica (2); and if the disc protrudes further, it may trap a nerve, causing great pain along the length of that nerve (3).

The disc is a self-contained fluid system that absorbs shocks. It only allows a small amount of compression, and because of the fluid displacement within the nucleus, allows easy movement to take place.

The disc separates the two adjacent vertebrae and prevents them from rubbing on each other. It also prevents pinching or compression of the spinal nerves as they protrude from between the two vertebrae.

If too much pressure is put on the disc, like any other body system, it will fail and tear or break. The layers of the outer case of the disc bulge or rupture, allowing the semi-fluid nucleus to leak into the crack created. If the outermost layer is still intact then there will be a bulge, just like the bulge on the wall of a car tyre. This is known as disc herniation. It can cause deep low backache, and typical pain and stiffness first thing in the morning as the spine takes the body weight after being horizontal all night. The stiffness is caused by the muscles around the weakened disc tightening up to protect it and to try to compensate for its injury.

Sometimes, the damage is very great, and the annulus actually ruptures or splits right through. Then a piece of the soft nucleus is squeezed out of the disc rather in the way that toothpaste is squeezed out of a tube. If it comes to rest against a nerve, it can trap or pinch it, causing severe pain, numbness or pins and needles down the buttock, legs, or even in the foot. This is called referred pain. The trapped nerve relays the pain sensation to the area of the body it controls. For example, pains in the leg and foot may be the result of a trapped sciatic nerve in the lowest region of the back.

Most herniated or even ruptured discs do very well without surgical treatment. Osteopaths can help in relieving the pressure and muscle spasm of the area, and so allow the disc to heal itself and become strong again. In acute cases, the osteopath would probably prescribe bed rest and treat the patient at home using gentle stretch techniques, so as to allow the bulge to be gradually reabsorbed.

Sometimes, however, the nerve root pressure is too strong or the patient is in danger of losing control of nerves to vital structures such as the bladder, or the bowels. In these cases, surgical removal of the disc altogether is indicated. The appropriate medical specialist should be consulted. It must be stressed that this is very rare and in many cases good osteopathic treatment can prevent surgery.

What the osteopath can do for the disc sufferer is to treat him or her after the acute attack has subsided so as to encourage rapid healing and help prevent a recurrence. It is very common to hear a patient say that he or she has suffered a grumbling disc lesion for many years. Very often it is because the factors that predisposed the disc to damage have not been dealt with adequately in the first place. Osteopathy is as much the science of finding out why the problem has occurred as it is the science of healing the damage, once it has been done.

Osteopathy in chronic disease

In chronic disease, part of the cure is to keep the tissue in question supplied with fresh oxygenated blood, so that it is able to repair itself to the best of its ability. If blood is allowed to pool in the peripheral tissue it will lead to a pre-pathological state and thus predispose the body to ill-health and disease. This means that the lungs and circulatory system must be in good order. That is why osteopaths place great importance on the ribs and diaphragm in the treatment of chronic disease.

The lungs are the organs that exchange waste gases for oxygen in the bloodstream. They are intimately connected with the cardiovascular system and the neuro-musculo-skeletal system. One of the earliest symptoms of heart disease is shortness of breath.

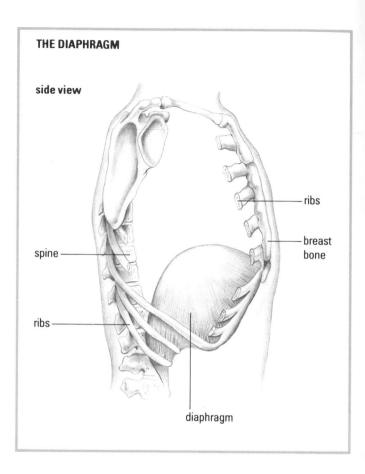

THE DIAPHRAGM

side view

ribs

breast bone

spine

ribs

diaphragm

The muscular sheet of the diaphragm attaches at the breastbone, ribs and low back. Osteopathic treatment at the points of attachment can help with respiratory problems and promote efficient breathing.

The diaphragm is a large sheet of muscle that divides the body in half, with the thoracic cavity above and the abdominal cavity below. It is attached in the front to the base of the breastbone (sternum), behind to the upper lumbar vertebrae, and all round to the ribs and rib cartilage. It is not the only respiratory muscle and it is helped by other muscles between the ribs, in the neck and back, in times of greater need.

Osteopathic treatment to stretch these points of attachment and normalize function in the ribs and thoracic spine both directly and via the spinal reflexes improve the tone of the diaphragm and give it a greater range of movement. It is the action of the diaphragm as it goes up and down like the piston in a pump that draws blood up into the chest from below and so good diaphragm movement aids venous return back to the heart from the abdomen, pelvis and lower limbs.

A wider view of osteopathic treatment

Dr Still foresaw osteopathy as a complete system of medicine. He may have been over-optimistic. In the United States, not all those who practise osteopathic medicine explore its full potential. However, as DOs sacrificed much of their purity for the right to practise like MDs, the purists among them can apply the principles of osteopathy to patients legally in all settings.

In the UK and Europe, osteopaths have a more restricted practice and some (though not all) DOs see osteopathy as largely limited to the treatment of degeneration and trauma within the NMS as a means of treating body disease. Taking the narrow view, osteopathy only treats a limited range of cases. The techniques are sophisticated and the results are good, but the treatment possibilities are only finite. In the broader view, osteopathy has the potential to approach body dysfunction from a much wider viewpoint, provided that both patient and therapist are prepared to accept a wider context for osteopathic diagnosis and technique.

There are many disease conditions in many different organ systems that are amenable to osteopathic treatment. There is a fine pathway linking disease and health and the movement along this pathway is in two directions. At which point does a disease begin? Exactly when does damage at the cellular level become irreversible? These are the fundamental questions for all in the healing arts. We should not be content to study the change that takes place in a diseased organ, but also the factors which push that organ towards disease and away from health. This pre-pathological state is amenable to change because the organ concerned has a blood and lymph supply and drainage system and is intimately connected with other organs and control systems through nerves. No organ exists alone. Every organ is capable of modification and change. Osteopathy maintains that organ dysfunction is amenable to adaptation and change through the nexus of the NMS.

By using the anatomical and physiological principles that exist within the body, osteopathy can be used to treat problems in the gastric system such as gastric reflux indigestion or constipation; in the respiratory system, to treat chronic asthma, bronchitis and emphysema; in the cardiovascular system, to treat poor peripheral circulation, hypertension (high blood pressure) and angina; and in the female reproductive system, to treat period pain and PMT. It has also proved useful for headaches, migraine and sinusitis.

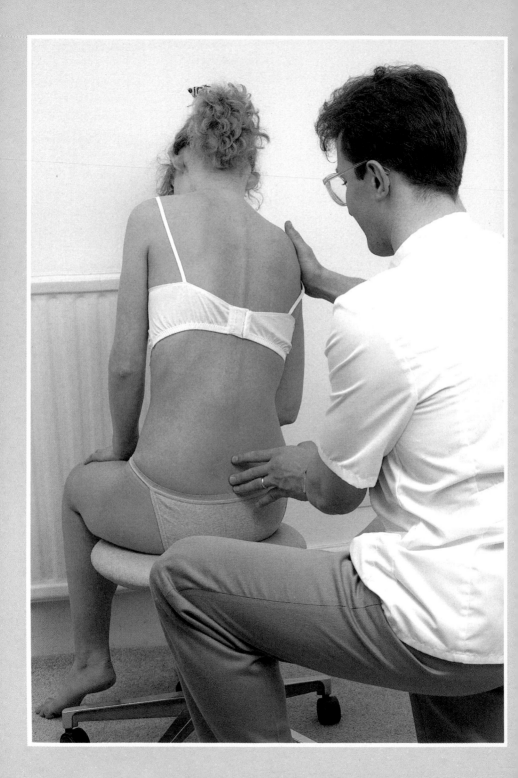

5

OSTEOPATHY IN ACTION

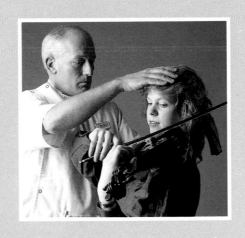

Although osteopaths are most often called upon in a crisis – when a patient is suffering from sudden, severe back pain, for instance – they are, in fact, primary care practitioners. This means that they are able to examine patients, make diagnoses, and prescribe safe treatment from a first contact with a patient. In the UK, there is no need to be referred to an osteopath by your family doctor, and in the United States, of course, your family doctor may well be a DO.

Training in osteopathy includes the basic sciences of anatomy (the study of the structure of the body), physiology (the functioning of the body), biochemistry (the internal workings of the body) and pathology (the nature and causes of disease). A thorough knowledge of these subjects enables osteopaths to recognize diseases and disorders in the human body. In particular, osteopathic training concentrates on detailed study of the human structure and its mechanics. Where the patient's condition indicates a different approach, the appropriate treatment will be given or the relevant specialist consulted.

Osteopaths need a working knowledge of other medical disciplines so that they can plan the course of treatment that is best suited to each individual patient. Practitioners are therefore trained in assessing faults in a patient's health, diagnosing abnormalities, and selecting appropriate techniques to correct (if possible) those faults they find. Naturally they are also fully schooled in the ethics of administering primary health care.

Consulting an osteopath

Usually, the first thing that makes someone decide to consult an osteopath for OMT is pain!

Most patients visit an osteopath on the recommendation of a friend, although the ever-increasing public awareness of the virtues of this type of treatment means that many patients come from other sources as well. Patients may also be referred or recommended by family doctors who do not themselves have any osteopathic training or qualifications.

In the past, one of the main difficulties encountered in orthodox medical diagnosis was the rigid idea that illness and health are definite, mutually exclusive states. A person was either healthy, in which case treatment was a waste of time, or not, in which case a disease could be diagnosed and treated. There could be no admission of a treatable in-between state.

This implied that if an illness couldn't be diagnosed it didn't exist. The possibility of intermediate states, such as mechanical disturbances in the working parts of an otherwise generally healthy body, was an idea that orthodox doctors found difficult to accept.

The minute disturbances which osteopaths refer to as 'osteopathic lesions' came into this intermediate category. They are difficult to feel using hands not trained in their subtleties, and they were thus often dismissed as a figment of the osteopath's imagination.

Now, however, the World Health Organization classification of illness includes a definition of 'somatic dysfunction' (an unwieldy term for mechanical breakdown) thereby recognizing at last one of the basic principles of osteopathic theory. With the ever-broadening of horizons, and increased awareness in the orthodox medical profession of the beneficial results of osteopathic treatment, scepticism about its effectiveness is now less of a problem.

It is easy to find an osteopath in the UK or USA by simply looking in the Yellow Pages under the appropriate listing. However the best form of research is to find a friend who can give you a personal recommendation. There is no better source of referral than from a satisfied patient.

The First Ten Questions All
of these questions are designed to discover the
structure causing the problem and what has hap-
pened to it, because structure governs function.

● What is the patient's
age / weight / job / sport or
hobby?
● Where is the site of the
pain?
● What sort of pain is it,
sharp or dull?
● How long have you had
it?
● How did it start, do you
remember doing any-
thing to start it off?
● What sort of thing makes
it worse?
● What sort of thing makes
it better?
● What other treatment
has the patient tried?
● Are they taking any
medication?
● Have they had any X-
rays or other hospital
tests and if so, what
were the results?

The importance of the case history

All medical practitioners, whatever their discipline, ask new patients to provide details of their medical history. Osteopaths are no exception. In fact, osteopaths usually take a particularly searching case history to identify the nature and type of the complaint, to consider any possible reasons (contra-indications) that might make osteopathy the wrong treatment, and to select the best approach for each individual case.

Taking a case history involves more than just collating large amounts of disconnected data. It enables the osteopath to piece together a diagnosis – the decision as to what is wrong – and to make a prognosis, deciding on the number of treatments, and the necessary time scale.

A detailed case history should also help to decide if the patient would be better off seeking treatment from some other therapy, or if the osteopath needs either another opinion or further tests to help determine the best approach. Taking the case history also introduces the patient to the practitioner, and helps him to understand the type of person he is dealing with and the way the patient relates to the problem.

While questioning the patient, the osteopath may seem to jump from one aspect of health to another, perhaps in a seemingly unrelated way. There are very good reasons for this, however, which should be clarified.

Modern osteopaths are trained in great depth to enable them to get from their patients as accurate a history as possible. Nevertheless, there is always the possibility that some patients, for various reasons, keep back certain facts and so make it difficult if not impossible to draw accurate conclusions. To get a complete picture of the patient's state of health the osteopath must also make a thorough physical examination in addition to the specific osteopathic palpatory (feeling with the hands) diagnosis.

Another reason for taking a careful and detailed case history is to differentiate between reality and imagination in a patient's view of their own problem. This is a particular problem with some patients who have musculo-skeletal disorders, because many of these are almost impossible to diagnose by conventional means. Consequently there is a tendency among orthodox doctors to regard their problems as entirely imaginary or 'psychosomatic'.

Such patients often find their way to osteopaths and, although it does happen that such patients tend to exaggerate the problem – probably because nobody seems to be taking

Taking a full case history is a very important part of the osteopathic procedure. People who have not consulted an osteopath before may be surprised at the depth and scope of the questioning, but rest assured that the osteopath needs to know as much about you as possible to make an accurate diagnosis of your problem and present a useful plan of recovery.

any notice or seems to understand – there is nearly always something wrong as well. Although the patient's description may be overemphasized, osteopathic diagnosis commonly reveals that a problem of some kind exists nevertheless.

A typical consultation

What does a visit to the osteopath entail? It may be helpful to visualize a specific case rather than generalize. Let us consider a woman who is suffering from pain in the shoulder and neck, and follow her progress from arrival at the osteopath's clinic through the whole procedure of taking the history, making an examination and giving a diagnosis, the first treatment and the arrangement of subsequent visits if necessary.

When the practitioner is ready to see the patient, she is shown into the consulting room. However this is furnished, it will always contain a treatment couch or table, which may be a fixed or hydraulic type. Some practitioners have a formal desk, whereas others use a chair and a clipboard, or merely sit on the side of the treatment table to go through the necessary questions for the case history.

Telling the 'story' The osteopath introduces himself, and puts the patient at ease by explaining the procedure and the way he works. Some patients are obviously nervous, and each practitioner has his own way of dealing with this problem. It is

If you use keyboards regularly — VDUs, word processors, computers or whatever — you will develop habits of posture that produce knots of tension. You may not feel them at first, but your osteopath will. That is why it is extremely useful for him to examine you while you are sitting in your normal work position.

perfectly natural to be fearful of the unknown. Some patients are anxious on first going to see any medical practitioner.

At the first visit it is not unusual for a patient to be in such acute pain with a locked joint or muscle spasm that the consultation has to be carried out with the patient lying down, or on all fours. Consultations have even been conducted with the patient stuck in the back of a car!

The preliminary questions relate to name, address, and so on. Then the patient is asked what she does for a living – and she explains that she is a secretary, spending much of her time at a typewriter keyboard. Merely knowing that she is a secretary is not enough, however. Some secretaries spend all day typing; others use a telephone much of the day; and still others do general clerical work. It is necessary to find out *precisely* what the patient does, so that the specific stresses on her body can be assessed and their relevance to her symptoms decided.

The patient is also asked about her sports or hobbies, because this can have a bearing on the physical state her body is in. It will also indicate how the pain is affected by different activities. For example, a woman who is keen on knitting is much more likely to have upper back and shoulder problems than someone who uses a sewing machine. This is because the relatively restricted movement of the arms in knitting tends to set up tension in the large muscles in the back of the neck, which often hurt if extra stress is placed upon them.

When he has an idea of how the patient uses her body in her daily routine, the osteopath moves on to the specific complaint.

Naturally, each practitioner places different importance on various aspects of the case history, and may ask questions in a different order, or ask additional questions. In this case, the patient explains that she has pain across the shoulders and upper back. Although the site of pain is of interest to the osteopath, the incidence and nature of the symptoms is of much greater relevance.

This part of the case history is known as the 'story'. Some patients are able to bring forward most of the points that the osteopath wants to ask. It is then fairly easy for him to elicit the relevant facts and fill in the gaps afterward with a few supplementary questions. Other patients answer only specific questions, and have to be led all the way. In either case, however, the osteopath should be able to find out what he needs to know, because he is trained to draw out the relevant details.

In this case the patient provides a 'story' of pain across the shoulders at the end of the day, followed by headaches. Because this is all she has mentioned, the therapist has to draw out the rest of the details he needs to make a decision as to whether he can treat her and if so, which of the many different osteopathic techniques might be appropriate.

By this stage of the case history, the osteopath will have assessed the patient's ability to answer questions accurately, and will have formed an opinion about her personality and her powers of observation. He will therefore be able to judge to what extent the verbal case history is going to be useful, and to what extent he will have to rely on the later physical examination.

The next line of questioning relates to the history of the problem since its onset. Has it got worse or better? Has there been a slow deterioration, or a gradual improvement? Has the situation been static and then suddenly changed in relation to particular physical, emotional or occupational stresses, or has there been any major change in the nature of the pain? He wants to know when the pain first started, whether it was sudden or slow in onset, and whether it is getting better or worse. The significance of the onset relates to the tissue from which the pain comes.

Many musicians consult osteopaths as a matter of routine. The strain on the joints and muscles is imposed by unnatural positions being held for long periods, leading to pain and discomfort.

Describing the symptoms There are often symptoms other than pain, which patients do not mention because they think they are irrelevant. However, any sensation a nerve can carry may be relevant including pain, pins and needles, numbness, a burning sensation and hypersensitivity. So-called 'motor' symptoms are of even greater importance. These include weakness in a limb and inability to perform normal movements.

Osteopaths are trained to understand the nature and behaviour of tissues in both health and disease. A knowledge of the way each tissue should perform, and how it is likely to behave in illness, can be helpful in identifying the series of clues that collectively lead to a diagnosis.

Each tissue of the body has specific symptoms relating to it. For example, arthritic pain is often worst if the joint has not been used for a while. This is also the case with muscle pain, but muscles usually loosen up after activity. An inflamed joint structure is irritated by heat, whereas an inflamed muscle can often be helped by the gentle application of heat. A strained ligament is immediately painful on stretching, whereas a muscle strain is painful at first and then becomes progressively easier.

The osteopath's next step is to find out what factors make the pain better or worse. In this case the patient explains that, although she has pain, it is not too bad at the moment of the consultation. It is interesting how often this occurs at a first consultation. The nervous stress of the visit to the osteopath may have been enough to override the pain, although if so, this relief will be only temporary.

The osteopath asks her *when* it is worse and when it is better. A common way of finding this out is to ask the patient to imagine a typical day. A question such as 'When is it worse?' is sometimes not easy to answer, whereas 'How are you when you wake up?' is much easier. 'How is the pain when you turn in bed? Or get up from bed? Or bend over the basin to wash?' and so on are much more helpful.

Case-history taking is both an art and a science. Carefully leading the patient in this way is perfectly acceptable, although it is important to avoid putting answers into the patient's mind. Too hasty questioning, or too influential prompting, can conceal far more than they reveal, because the osteopath is liable to get the answers he wants, rather than the answers that he needs to make an objective diagnosis.

In the case of this patient, questioning has revealed that the pain is worse toward the end of the afternoon and into the early evening. This seems to fit the pattern of a postural problem producing muscle fatigue at the end of typing sessions. Naturally there are many other possible causes which need to be considered, but this is a start.

Treatment selection As a general rule, pain originating in the structural tissues of the body is sooner or later modified in some way by movement, changes in posture, or simply by time. An osteopath is therefore always suspicious of pain that is not affected by one or more of these, because it may be a symptom of disease rather than a structural or mechanical problem. An awareness of this underlies the second main reason for taking a detailed case history – finding out whether or not disease is a possible cause.

The patient knows that she has a pain. Her friend has been to an osteopath and obtained considerable relief for an apparently similar condition and has recommended that she goes for a consultation and treatment. She has not seen her own family practitioner, and has not had any medical investigations. The osteopath will be open to the fact that any one of a number of diseases could possibly be causing her symptoms.

Violinist's neck He presents with his problem after spending the last two weeks working very hard learning and practising a new piece for a forthcoming music exam. When his osteopath examines him, he finds a chronic postural strain causing muscular pain which is aggravated by the repeated trauma of the poor head position Peter adopts when playing. This is opposite to his normal, healthy posture and thus causes neck strain and pain.

A fully trained osteopath has a thorough understanding of the processes of disease and should be able to differentiate between symptoms coming from the moving parts, and symptoms coming from the organs or other vital structures, which may need other types of treatment.

For example, take the case of pain affecting the right shoulder. One cause might be called 'referred pain', which does not actually come from the shoulder itself, but instead is 'referred' to the shoulder from an inflamed gall bladder. There would also be other symptoms to support this diagnosis and an osteopath is trained to recognize them. In such a case, treatment to the shoulder would be useless and, more seriously, might delay treatment to the underlying disorder.

Working with your family doctor In the US, a patient whose family doctor is not a DO might decide to consult a DO with a view to osteopathic manipulative therapy. In such cases patients might like their family doctors to be kept informed of their progress. In the UK, family doctors and osteopaths are separate. In both situations, assuming that the patient has not mentioned it earlier, the osteopath will also ask about the results of any previous treatment, medical or 'alternative'. He will also ask about her family doctor and whether he or she has been consulted.

Many general practitioners adopt a more or less passive approach to physical aches and pains, on the assumption that most will sooner or later disappear of their own accord whatever one does. There are in fact quite good reasons for this. A large proportion of common musculo–skeletal aches and pains do clear up without specific treatment, apart perhaps from simple painkilling drugs. Surveys have shown that something like 80 per cent of patients experience spontaneous improvement within a month. From the doctor's point of view, therefore, it makes sense to temporize for a while. Inevitably, however, some patients see this as time–wasting or uncaring and decide to seek help elsewhere.

On the other hand, a different perspective emerges from surveys of osteopathic practices, which reveal that a high percentage of patients consult an osteopath only after they have suffered from the problem for a month or more, sometimes as much as several months. This seems to suggest that in many cases the osteopath is working on conditions that are not naturally self-limiting.

If the osteopath knows the patient's family doctor, he will

probably ask the patient's permission to write to him to keep him informed about what is happening. If the osteopath and the doctor have a rapport they can work together for the benefit of the patient.

Unfortunately, in the UK, because of the different status of osteopathy, not all doctors agree with their patients consulting an osteopath. A doctor is always at liberty to recommend any course of treatment by any other practitioner that he feels may help in a particular case. There are, however, two essential conditions. First, the doctor must be assured of the competence of any other practitioner he recommends; and second, the doctor must retain overall authority in the case.

The first condition is assured in the UK with members of the Register of Osteopaths, who comply with a full code of professional ethics and conduct. But the second may be more of a problem, because if the patient's doctor sends a patient to an osteopath who performs some treatment that causes damage, in law the doctor is liable. Naturally no doctor is keen to take such a risk. Even though the safety record of registered osteopaths is very good, therefore, many doctors feel unable to co-operate with another professional over whom they have no direct control.

Another consideration in the UK is directly related to the medical system. A patient 'belongs' to his or her general practitioner. This means that if patients wish to see another doctor or specialist, they must be referred by their family doctor. In practice this may not happen, but it is nevertheless the established system. Osteopaths commonly see their patients without any referral at all, however, and this sometimes angers a family doctor, who may feel his position is being undermined.

In the UK, osteopathic treatment is at present not available on the National Health Service, and therefore most osteopaths advise their patients to complete any course of National Health treatment that has already begun. After such treatment, if the results have not been satisfactory, an osteopath will then be willing to start any investigation or treatment necessary.

If a patient does decide to attend an osteopath for treatment, many hospitals are prepared to let the osteopath see copies of X-ray results, blood tests, and so on because this helps in the diagnosis and avoids the cost of repeating the investigations. X-rays are not only expensive, they expose the patient to a certain amount of radiation, which is best kept to the lowest level possible.

DOs and MDs American DOs have equal practising rights with MDs in every state of the union and in the District of Columbia. The granting of full practice rights including the prescribing and administration of drugs and performing surgery with instruments first took place in Audrain County in 1950. In 1963, DOs were accepted by the civil service as medical officers. In 1967, they were accepted as medical officers in the armed forces and in 1973 grainted full practice rights in every state.

Breathless Mrs C is an overweight 50-year-old complaining of not being able to catch her breath. When questioned closely, she reveals that this condition has been getting worse in the last two years since her menopause. It is so bad at the moment that she cannot climb two flights of stairs at work without pausing for a minute at the top.

Before approaching this problem from a musculo-skeletal point of view the osteopath will want to exclude other causes. His examination will consider problems in the heart and lungs, hypertension, bronchitis and emphysema, as well as conditions such as diabetes or thyroid problems which can come on after the menopause for the first time and present with breathlessness. Anaemia or a problem with the oxygen carrying capacity of the blood can lead to a shortness of breath too, and so before simply telling the patient to lose weight, or assuming that she has a problem with her ribs or muscular system, an osteopath has to exclude disease as a possible cause for this seemingly innocuous symptom.

Background information Once the osteopath has found out from the patient what investigations and treatments have already been carried out and what their results were, he will move on to questions relating to general health.

The patient's general health usually has a direct bearing on their problem. For example, the headaches that the patient experiences at the end of the afternoon may be caused by a condition of lowered blood sugar called hypoglycaemia. This means that the energy-producing part of food is being used up faster than it is being replaced, so the level of sugar (glucose) in the blood drops. This results in hunger, thirst, or in some cases headaches.

The osteopath's questions are directly related to the various systems of the body. He includes questions concerning the gastro-intestinal system (digestion and defaecation), the genito-urinary system (the sex organs, kidneys and bladder), the endocrine system (hormones), the circulatory system (heart, blood and circulation), the respiratory system (breathing) and the nervous system. He will ask simple questions relating to each system to ensure that everything is functioning normally. If anything is not functioning as it should, he will ask more questions, delving deeper into the problem. In this way the osteopath may also discover if there are other aspects of the patient's health that osteopathy might be able to benefit.

In the case in question, the osteopath finds that the patient gets slightly out of breath when climbing stairs. She attributes this to having put on weight over recent years since the birth of her daughter, and to getting too little exercise in her sedentary job.

Both these facts may seem unrelated to the patient's headaches, yet this information may be significant. For example, while she is sitting for several hours a day at her typewriter she is leaning forward slightly, so her recent weight gain puts an increased strain on the delicate shoulder muscles.

The fact that the patient gets breathless when climbing stairs also may not at first seem to connect with her neck problem. Nevertheless, breathlessness implies the use of the secondary respiratory muscles, which are the powerful muscles in the root of the neck designed to assist in lifting the rib cage for deep breathing. If they are overworking, they may put additional strain on the neck which can lead to discomfort and inefficient working of the muscles – a disturbance of function that can result in pain.

Medical history The next set of questions relates to any past medical conditions. There are two main reasons for this part of the case history. The first is to find out if there are any contra-indications to any particular types of osteopathic procedures, perhaps because of weakness of the underlying structures due to previous surgery, disease or degeneration. The second is to find out if there is any reason to suggest sending the patient on for further investigation or for examination by another practitioner.

Previous surgery can have a major effect on the way the body works, because scar tissue can alter body mechanics quite significantly. Long-term medication with certain drugs can alter responses to physical treatment, and some drugs do in fact have very serious side-effects on certain structures in the body. The osteopath needs to know which drugs (if any) the patient is taking for other reasons as well.

There are many good reasons why the doctor in charge of a case may not have told the patient everything about their condition and its treatment. But if the osteopath is to gain a complete picture, he must know as much as possible. If it is not possible to get the necessary information, however, merely the name of any drugs used can give the osteopath a good idea of the nature of the problem.

In the case under review, the osteopath learns that the patient had an operation for a bunion about a year ago, and she recalls that the slight neck discomfort she suffered originally became worse after that time. This is by no means uncommon. The distorted walking pattern following an operation on the foot often tips the balance (in a mechanical sense) of a body from a situation where compensation is just about possible to one where it is not.

Everyone has slightly asymmetrical bones, joints and muscles. This is normal, and so is the body's ability to adapt and compensate for these slight variations without problems. Many patients who consult an osteopath have slight structural abnormalities of this kind which have been irritated or aggravated by some superimposed strain. The treatment is not to the 'abnormality' itself, however, but to the inappropriate adaptation processes.

In fact it is not unusual to experience some degree of neck discomfort after surgery on any part of the body. When a patient is sedated on the operating table, a tube is passed down the throat to ease breathing, to prevent the tongue from being swallowed, and to ensure the anaesthetic gases reach deep into

The long and the short of it
It is extremely rare to come across a patient who does not have one leg shorter than the other. Just as we rarely have two feet or hands of the same size or two breasts of the same size, so the human frame has differences in leg length. It is when the compensation for this leg length difference breaks down that we have problems.

the lungs. If the neck is pushed back a long way to ease the passage of this tube, a neck disorder can and often does ensue. After the operation, discomfort in the neck is ignored as much more important things are considered. Nevertheless the neck can still hurt long after the surgical wound has healed.

Summary   In this case, the patient is an essentially healthy woman who is complaining of discomfort in the lower neck and mild headaches at the end of working sessions at the typewriter. She admits to being a little overweight and unfit. She has reasonable general health and has no medical history of any consequence except a bunion operation a year ago. She experiences an increase of pain in her neck at the end of the day and when she has remained static for a period. This pain is relieved by rest, simple painkillers and applying heat to her neck.

She has made arrangements to have an X-ray, which revealed nothing much apart from normal, mild 'wear and tear'. She has been advised to take some painkillers if the pain becomes a problem, and to wait and see if her condition improved. She was not entirely happy with this situation, and when a friend mentioned that she had been to an osteopath for a similar problem, she thought she would visit him too, to see if he could help.

In this case history there are no obvious reasons for the osteopath to avoid treating the patient so, after a few further questions to clarify certain points, he leaves the room while she removes her top clothing in preparation for the next stage, the examination.

The physical examination
In the first part of the examination, the osteopath asks the patient to stand so that he can look at her posture from the front, the back and the sides. The purpose of this general physical examination is to give the osteopath an overall picture of the state of balance in the tissues and the type of compensation patterns that have been established over a period of time. He will be looking particularly for any irregular curves in the spine and any obvious discrepancies in length between the hips and knees and the knees and ankles.

Movement   After making notes and sometimes diagrams of the body's structure, the osteopath asks the patient to perform some simple movements. This normally includes bending

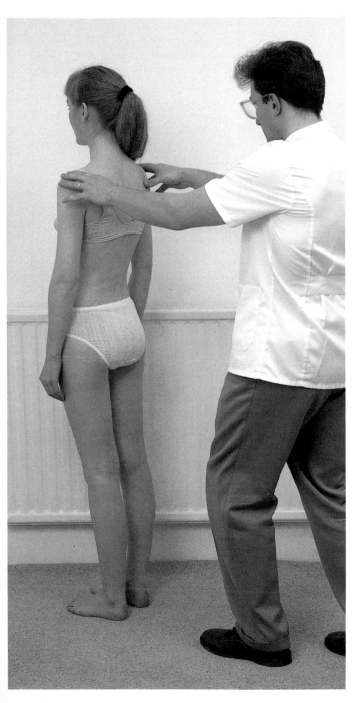

After taking exhaustive case notes, the osteopath will as a matter of course, assess your posture and check that your spine is straight and your shoulders are level. Here he is placing his fingers on the shoulder blade (scapula) on each side to see that they line up.

forward and backward, bending to each side and turning to each side. This tells him about the range and to some extent the quality of the movement of the body as a whole. The osteopath is particularly interested in the behaviour of the part of the body where the pain is located, and the way the patient moves that part in relation to other parts. The way a part of the body moves and co-operates with movement of the whole body is particularly important to the diagnosis of mechanical problems.

There are many tests that the osteopath can carry out on the body; naturally they are not all appropriate to every case. In one important test, the patient is asked to stand on one foot for a short while. This tests balance, muscle strength, and foot, leg

Continuing the postural assessment, the osteopath checks how the spine behaves when the body is twisted to the right or left, to see if it distorts or if movement is restricted in any direction.

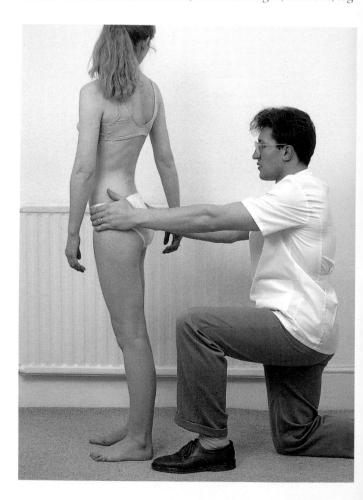

and hip function. In another test the patient stands with both feet parallel and then lets one knee drop. This shows a trained observer how the spine and pelvis work together. If the spine bends more to one side than the other, there is a distinct possibility of either a difference in leg lengths, or of some unusual configuration in the structure of the spine.

Almost half the population has a measurable difference in the length of the legs. In itself this does not cause any problems, except when the ability of the body to compensate has been disturbed and discomfort ensues. The compensation mechanism takes the form of altered posture, side-bending curves in the spine, and a tendency to slump to one side. Many people do this to a small extent and have no symptoms. When symptoms

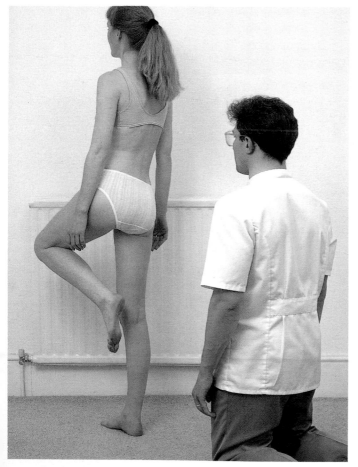

As a third part of the assessment, the osteopath checks balance, observing the degree of muscle strength in the legs, how the foot and hip function as a unit, and how the rest of the body behaves when it is compensating during the temporary removal of one support.

Amazingly, nearly half the population has one leg shorter than the other, giving rise to many niggling problems and generalized back pain.

There are four points along the leg to check for equal length: the hips, knees, ankles and feet. The shortfall could be at any of these points. The first check is at the pelvis. The osteopath checks by eye and by palpating the haunches (iliac crests) to make sure that the hips are in alignment.

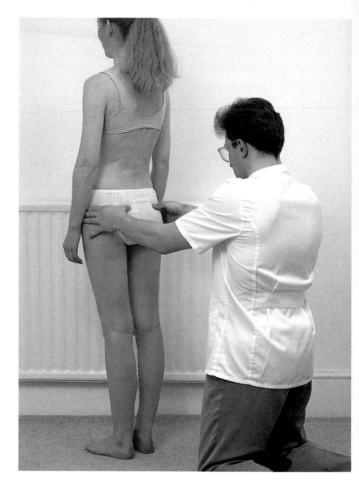

do occur, however, and an osteopath is consulted, the situation is usually quite far developed. There are then likely to be several layers of compensation to undo.

A common way of compensating for a difference in leg lengths is for the lower spine to curve toward the shorter side. This tends to produce a secondary curve in the middle of the back, and there is often a third curve even higher in the upper back or neck. In many cases the lower curves cause little problem: the discomfort appears in the neck because of the inability of the body to adapt to the multiple curves, or because of some minor strain that the body cannot resolve. Treating the local pain when the cause is elsewhere in the structure of the body only provides temporary relief. This is

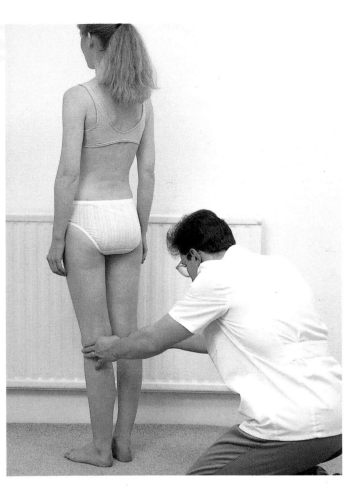

The next check is at knee level. This is not done at the kneecaps, which are extremely mobile and therefore unreliable as a measure, but the tops of the fibula in each leg. (The fibula is the long bone which runs down the outside curve of the leg.) The fibula is not a weight-bearing bone, but it is an important anchorage for many muscles, all of which could cause problems.

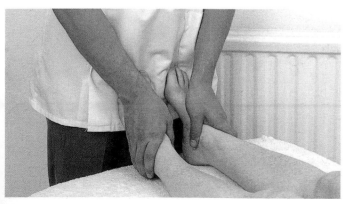

The last check is made with the patient lying down so that gravity or posture distortions can be ruled out. The osteopath compares the legs at ankle level and looks at the arches of the feet.

why osteopaths always examine the patient's whole body, not just the painful part.

Next, the osteopath asks his patient to walk up and down slowly so that he can assess the overall mobility of her body and its efficiency in motion. He observes that she has a foot problem, which she forgot to mention at the beginning of the consultation, but which completely distorts her walking pattern and therefore the way her pelvis moves in relation to the legs and the rest of the spine.

This part of the examination is attempting to build up a picture of what is 'normal' for the patient, and why her normal condition has undergone changes that now seem to be causing her pain.

The osteopath will also want to see the body in action, to assess any postural difficulties or problems in your normal walking position.

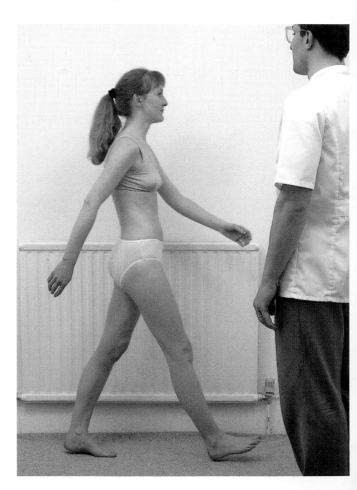

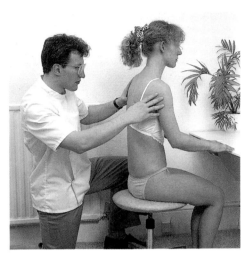

Posture To examine posture, the patient is asked first to sit, either on the treatment table or on a chair. The osteopath notes the way she moves when she changes posture, and this also helps him in completing a picture of her body as a functioning mechanical unit. While examining her, he continues to ask questions, and observes her manner of answer to assess the way she relates to her pain. Some people have a high pain tolerance and make little fuss even in severe situations; others are just the opposite. An osteopath is trained to make an assessment of a person on the basis of verbal and non-verbal responses, which reflect the whole person, as well as looking on a patient as a collection of moving parts.

In this case, the osteopath observes his patient's sitting posture especially carefully. Because her symptoms relate to sitting, he is particularly interested in whether she sits well or badly.

It is difficult to define 'good' posture although it is not difficult to see 'bad' posture! A good posture can be looked upon as one which uses the minimum energy to relate to the environment and which is most efficient in performing the task in hand at any one time.

The osteopath is also interested in the way she carries her head in relation to the neck, and whether the eyes are held level. Many patients with visual disturbances suffer from discomfort in the neck and head. This is sometimes caused by 'eye-strain', but more commonly by holding the head in a distorted posture – perhaps in an attempt to see better despite

Finally, it is useless for the osteopath to examine you doing everything but what you do most of the time, namely your job. If your job involves sitting at a keyboard, he will ask you to recreate your actions there and palpate various areas of the body while .you 'work' to see what effect your action is having on them.

Of course it will not be of much significance if you only sit at a keyboard or a telephone for short intervals, but a whole working day spent in front of the VDU or crouched over the telephone can engender bad postural habits such as crossing the legs (above) and clamping the telephone to your ear by bending your neck unnaturally.

slight difficulties. If an eye problem is suspected the patient would be referred to an ophthalmologist.

While the patient is sitting, the osteopath checks her active movements again. These are the movements she can perform on request, such as bending forward or sideways.

Palpation

The next stage of the examination is palpation, feeling with the hands. An osteopath spends most of his time working with his hands, and develops a very refined sense of touch that enables him to assess normal and abnormal tissue states by feel. He would be particularly interested in the muscles and joints in the back of the patient's neck and shoulder girdles, but would probably extend his examination down as far as the lower back joints and pelvis.

Once he has a good idea of the location of areas of tenderness, irritability or poor function, he proceeds to movement testing. Osteopathic movement testing takes several forms. The most common involves passive movement. This means that the osteopath says something like 'I am going to move your neck in different directions. I want you to let me do the moving, but tell me if any of these movements are painful.' He then repeats all the movements that the patient carried out herself for the preceding examination of movement, but guides them with his hands and senses the movement with his trained touch to detect any abnormalities. Tenderness by itself is not a complete guide to the site of a problem.

Static palpation and palpation of movement patterns may then be followed by palpation of changes in posture. For example, the osteopath may ask the patient to put her arms in the position in which she holds them when typing and then make some typing movements. While this is going on, he feels the state of tension or otherwise in the muscles at the back of her neck.

By now the therapist has formed a fairly full opinion about the mechanical state of the patient's tissues and possible reasons why they might have broken down and caused the symptoms she is complaining of. He will then put her in various different positions to palpate the tissues and structures in the neck and upper back. Common examination positions are lying down on the back, on the left or right side, and lying face-down. In the face-down position, pillows are used to support the abdomen and prevent pressure on the chest.

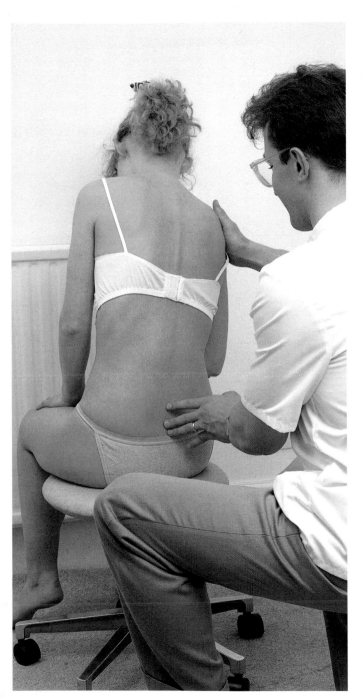

After examining you for the most part by looking, the osteopath moves on to palpation. A great deal of osteopathic training is taken up learning how to read information from the body through the hands. An osteopath should know immediately whether the message from the tissue has changed. Here he is using passive articulation, pushing the patient forward gently while palpating to see what effect the movement is having.

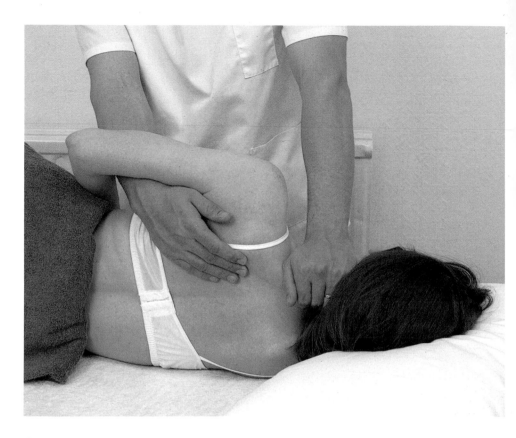

A very common site for injury and problems is the neck and shoulder area; here palpation is used to assess the state of the neck muscles. Palpation is also used after a technique has been carried out to monitor the response.

'Mechanical' diagnosis

The mechanical diagnosis is made from a combination of history, examination and palpation. A thorough case history gives a complete guide for diagnosis; the examination leads to a confirmed diagnosis; and the palpatory assessment confirms the diagnosis in a mechanical sense. In theory, it should be possible for three different osteopaths to perform the three different functions and come to the same conclusions. In practice, of course, this would be very unusual, but it is done as an academic exercise during osteopathic training to prove the point.

Medical examination

The order in which the various tests take place is left to the individual practitioner. There is one further thing he needs to do to assure himself of the true nature of the case, however. This is to perform a medical examination.

In an average osteopath's practice relatively few serious diseases are encountered, but he must always remain alert to the possibility nevertheless.

Not every patient needs a full medical examination. If a footballer comes in with a sprained ankle, no more than a brief check-up is necessary. The case of our hypothetical patient is, however, somewhat different. Her symptoms could come from a brain or spinal tumour at worst, or a lesser condition of high blood pressure or hormone imbalance. She might be suffering from eye strain, stress, bad lighting at work or simply a postural problem. It is essential for the osteopath to know which.

In this case, as additional tests, the osteopath would measure the patient's blood pressure and look into her eyes using an ophthalmoscope. In view of her slight breathlessness, he would also listen to her lungs and heart. In certain cases an osteopath also requires tests of blood or urine, and X-rays are taken in about 15 to 20 per cent of new patient consultations.

X-rays are used for two main purposes: to exclude the likelihood of bone disease; and to assist in the detection of bone or joint anomaly or abnormality. Sometimes 'moving' X-ray films are used to assist in the diagnosis of 'hypermobile' or excessively mobile segments in the spine.

Osteopaths use X-rays in approximately 20 per cent of cases. The first view on the left is of the head and neck looking from the side. Apart from looking for any disease or trauma, the osteopath looks for the front to back curve of the neck and at the small joints between the cervical vertebrae.

In the view on the right, the lower spine and pelvis are viewed from front to back. The osteopath is looking again for curves, but this time from side to side. He also looks at the disc spaces to see if there is an inference of the thinning of the discs.

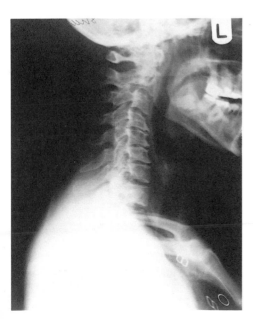

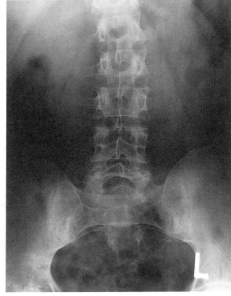

Diagnosis

What has the osteopath found in the hypothetical patient's case? She is a middle-aged woman suffering from upper back and lower neck discomfort. She also gets a headache from it toward the end of the working day. She types most of the day in an office under fluorescent light and is a little overweight and breathless on exertion.

His findings on examination show that she tends to be a little kyphotic (round-shouldered) and that she has an area of increased muscle tension across the upper back and lower neck. She carries her head a little forward of the body, putting more tension on the neck muscles than is necessary, and carries her head slightly to one side. She favours the right eye, which seems stronger than the left. She has normal blood pressure and on examination the retina of the eye seems normal. She wears spectacles but has not had them checked for several years. Heart sounds are normal and the lungs seem clear.

Her lower neck muscles are very tight and there is an area of almost complete loss of mobility between the fifth and sixth neck (cervical) vertebrae on both sides. The upper cervical vertebrae have very limited mobility, particularly the movement of the second against the third, which seems to be twisted slightly to the left.

The initial conclusion is that the patient has a simple posturo-mechanical strain of the joints and muscles in the base of the neck secondary to slight overweight, poor postural adaptation to the working environment. There is also a degree of unfitness in the muscles, which aggravates the postural imbalance.

Prognosis and treatment

The final, and most difficult, part of the consultation is the prognosis. Prognosis predicts the result of the treatment and how long it will take.

It is easy to give a guarded prognosis and tell the patient that it will be a 'long job' – but this is hardly helpful. Most patients want to know how long treatment needs to go on, as well as how much it will cost them and whether the condition can be cleared, cured, or merely alleviated.

Many conditions can be completely cleared up, although the word 'cure' is rarely used. For many of the mechanical problems osteopathy tackles, the idea of a definitive 'cure' is not really appropriate, because of the many reasons why these problems arose in the first place. There are also, unfortunately,

Tension headaches Headaches are a common problem that the osteopath is called upon to treat. Once he has ruled out any pathological cause and established whether or not the patient has recently had an eye-test, he looks at the musculo-skeletal system. The short, tight muscles that attach the neck to the skull link with a cap of muscles that go right over the head and increased tension in the muscles under the skull can cause a 'cap' like headache which responds very well to osteopathic treatment.

a number of conditions in which it is possible only to get partial relief, or where the relief is temporary. If this is explained carefully, most patients suffering from such complaints are pleased to accept a temporary relief, with periodic check-ups to keep them going for extended periods.

The timing of these check-ups inevitably varies according to the particular condition: many cases need only an annual session; some need monthly attention; but rarely is a more frequent maintenance schedule practical, economical or indeed wise, although there are of course exceptions.

In our hypothetical case, the osteopath would expect to be able to help his patient, over a course of some four to six sessions. For best results, she would have to follow other more general advice he proposed as well, such as visiting an ophthalmologist and updating her spectacles prescription; beginning a sensible diet, to get her weight down to the optimum level; and taking gentle exercise, to maintain muscle tone generally (although this would probably be left until all physical treatment had been completed satisfactorily).

Principles of treatment

Osteopathic treatment consists of well documented and defined techniques which can be reliably taught and reproduced. Trained osteopathic students have undergone many hours of this 'technique' teaching. In fact, much of the practice is done on each other so that all students, and therefore all qualified practitioners, have been manipulated many more times than their patients ever will be.

The actual techniques themselves are put together in the order and intensity that the practitioner considers appropriate to the particular case. Herein lies one very important aspect of the 'art' of osteopathy, rather than the science.

The use of manipulation is as old as recorded history, being documented from the earliest writings. The particular types of manipulative techniques used by osteopaths are highly refined and rely on a thorough understanding of the underlying anatomy of the body and a unique sympathy with varying tissue states in health and disease.

The term 'tissue dialogue' is used to denote the process of 'requesting' information from the tissues and then directing the forces in treatment to the answers to these questions.

The techniques used by modern osteopaths fall into three broadly overlapping groups. These are: rhythmic techniques; thrust techniques; and low-velocity stress techniques.

Rhythmic techniques

The techniques that together are described as 'rhythmic' techniques include a number of different skills and approaches. There are eight principal ones:

1	Kneading	5	Inhibition
2	Stretching	6	Effleurage
3	Articulation	7	Vibration
4	Springing	8	Rhythmic traction

Springing is one of the rhythmic techniques. This is a kind of bouncing movement of the osteopath's hands over certain areas of the body (here to the mid thoracic spine). The cushion under the chest is to prevent undue pressure on the abdomen.

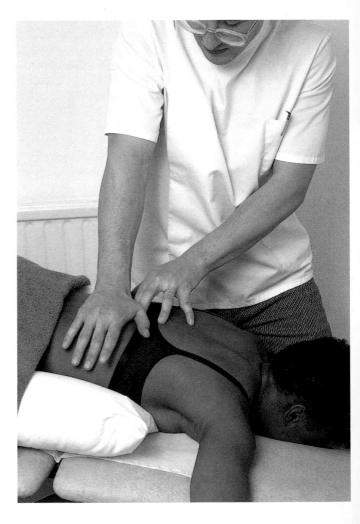

Osteopaths vary their techniques to suit the patient and his or her condition, however, and it is this that makes each treatment a unique experience.

Each of these terms is in fact best understood in terms of the technique the osteopath is applying, rather than what he is trying to achieve. For example, when a part of the body is moved steadily in a particular direction, the technique can be described as stretching. If the osteopath takes a comfortable hold on the patient and pulls intermittently he can be seen to be applying rhythmic traction. If he takes a joint and its surrounding structures and passively (i.e. without the patient taking an active part, other than co-operating) moves it through a range of movement he is 'articulating' it.

It can be seen from this that the classification of rhythmic techniques has been chosen to describe the application of forces to the body rather than any supposed action of those forces. This type of classification is easier to communicate and to teach, and also aids dialogue between disciplines.

Thrust techniques

The second category of osteopathic techniques is divided according to subtly different characteristics.

1   Combined leverage and thrust.
2   Momentum-induced leverage and thrust.
3   Minimal leverage and thrust.
4   Non-leverage and thrust.
5   Non-leverage and thrust using momentum.

Once again, the names reflect the descriptions of the techniques, rather than rigidly defining the many different ways that the osteopath can apply these techniques.

Thrust techniques used to be called 'specific correction or adjustment techniques'. It is now known that the point of thrust techniques is not to 'correct' anything, but merely to mobilize. In fact, the modern approach to these techniques is to use the lowest possible force that is consistent with achieving the required results of increased mobility, improved function and lessened pain.

Thrust techniques are the ones that lay people most commonly associate with osteopathy. Unfortunately, the equally common idea that an osteopath merely clicks a few

The technique most associated with osteopathy in the lay mind is undoubtedly the thrust technique. There are many kinds of thrusts, one of the most used being the High Velocity Thrust on the lumbar (low back) spine to mobilize a specific joint lesion in the spine.

bones and the patient leaps off the table, miraculously cured of all ills, is not always the case! Most osteopaths can tell stories of 'miracle' cases, but these are the exception rather than the rule. The majority of osteopathic treatment consists of coaxing normal movement back into stiffened and rigid tissues so that the body can get on with using its own maintenance and repair mechanisms. The gentle, accurate, osteopathic thrust technique is a perfect example of this type of process in action.

The classical thrust is a very short, sharp movement performed very fast to release adhering joint surfaces. It is often accompanied by a 'crack' or 'pop'. It should not be painful and in fact many patients seem to like to hear this sound as an indication that something has been done. Many osteopathic treatments do not in fact need the thrust, however, and whether or not it is used depends on the needs of the tissues at the time.

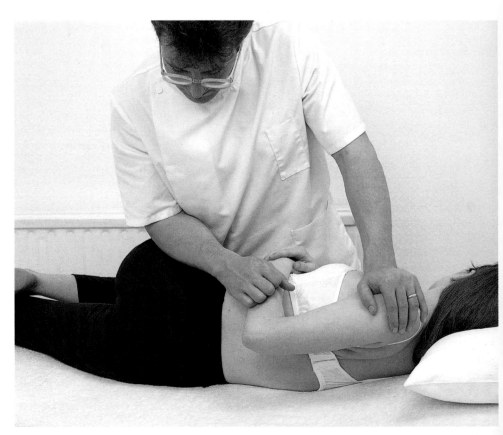

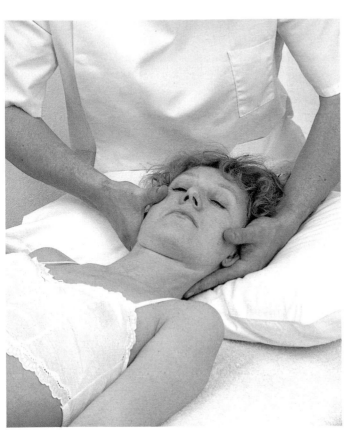

Another High Velocity Thrust (HVT), this time to the neck, to mobilize it. HVTs are quick, short and sharp and do not hurt. The pop that you might hear is the bursting of CO_2 gas inside the joint capsules.

Low-velocity stress techniques

The third category includes the following procedures:

1 Low velocity stress with sustained pressure.
2 Low velocity stress with sustained levers.
3 Low velocity stress with sustained traction.
4 Low velocity stress with sustained articulation.

Low-velocity stress techniques are applied slowly and for quite a long time, using the absolute minimum of force to achieve a gradual release of tension in body structures. They are gentle release techniques and also the true 'tissue dialogue' techniques referred to on p. 105. They take tension out of tissues and produce a state of calm and rest and relaxation.

To some, low-velocity stress techniques seem almost like 'laying on of hands'. However, spiritual healing whatever its merits, does not really relate to osteopathic treatment – although there is always likely to be an element of the 'therapeutic touch' in any system that relies on the application of the hands to the body. Low velocity stress techniques are more involved with taking energy out than putting it in.

There are also various specialized methods of osteopathic treatment, which tend either to be named after their inventors, or to have other specific names. They include functional technique, positional release technique, specific adjusting technique, muscle energy technique and cranial technique.

Cranio-sacral techniques

Cranial osteopathy is a specialized form of osteopathic techniques which follows the teaching of Dr William Garner Sutherland (see p. 140). Sutherland discovered that the bones of the skull are not fixed, but can move slightly. Although the degree of movement is very small, it can be measured by an oscilloscope under laboratory conditions and can be detected by the trained palpating hand.

Inside the skull, the brain is suspended by sheets of fascial tissue known as the meninges, that are held in tension by their bony attachments. The meninges extend all the way down the vertebral column to the sacrum at the base of the spine.

This linkage provides a system called a reciprocal tension mechanism, which connects the movement of the skull bones and the movement of the sacrum. The fascia is attached at one end in the skull and at the other in the pelvis.

Osteopaths who have studied and specialized in this system maintain that palpation on the skull and sacrum can pick up a rhythmic pulsation distinct from the respiratory rhythm or the heartbeat and pulse of the blood. This pulsation is the reverberation of the cerebrospinal fluid, which bathes both the brain and the spinal column. This is the CRI or Cranial Rhythmic Impulse.

Each cranial bone moves along a set axis guided by its articulation with its neighbours; any disturbance of the normal cranial bone movement will lead to a corresponding disturbance of the normal cranial rhythm and thus disturb the normal fluid flow. Cranio-sacral techniques use these disturbed patterns of movement to diagnose and treat all sorts of disorders in a gentle non-invasive way, and the effects of this treatment can be very far-reaching. Cranial work tries to balance the rhythmical forces at work in the body by gently guiding and releasing the tensions within the tissues.

Children in particular respond well to the gentle approach that this form of treatment offers: babies only a few days old can be treated with this technique for simple birth trauma (see also p. 44).

Treatment in practice

Having established the range of different types of procedures available, let us see how they can be applied in the case of the hypothetical patient.

It has been established that the neck is the prime source of symptoms and that severe disease has been excluded.

So the osteopath's treatment plan would probably start with work directly on the sensitive muscles across the shoulders and lower neck. This will be followed by some gentle but firm stretching applied to these muscles and the underlying joints, which feel stiff and painful at the end of the day. If any joints really resist this stretching process, some gentle thrust techniques will be applied to free them.

The first session

On the first visit, the patient is asked to lie face down with a pillow under her abdomen to prevent excessive pressure on the chest. The osteopath will start with a technique that will relax the patient, giving her confidence, and will also give him a feel for the tissues.

In this case it would be the kneading technique applied to the muscles of the shoulders and root of the neck. This would be done slowly and with gradually increasing pressure until he feels the muscles begin to relax.

Once he has gained some relaxation in this way, the osteopath would probably move on to the rhythmic techniques called springing. This is designed to loosen tight joints and improve the quality as well as the quantity of their movement. After a few moments of this – once again when he has sensed a change in the tissue mobility – he would ask the patient to turn on to one side.

In the side-lying position there are many techniques that can be used to reach the muscles at the root of the neck and across the shoulders. The osteopath would probably also work on the shoulder joints themselves to ensure free mobility.

After work had been done on both sides, the patient would be asked to turn on to her back, and the osteopath would once

The truth about double joints There is no such thing as someone who is double jointed. We are all born with the same number of joints. However, some people are very mobile and this gives them a greater range of movement which makes them think they have an extra joint. Usually this is a harmless condition, but sometimes it is due to a problem with the ligaments and can cause pain if the joints are overstrained.

again work on the shoulder joints and the collar bone attachments to the shoulders before moving on to the neck itself. Standing at the head of the table he would work on the muscles of the neck, noting any particularly sensitive areas, any areas of tension in the muscles, and any restriction of mobility in the underlying joints.

If at this point the osteopath discovers one joint in particular which is so severely restricted that it resists his attempts to mobilize it using articulation, he would perform a thrust technique to speed up the process. Having carefully moved the neck so that the joints that need to be mobilized are correctly positioned to receive the thrust, he will warn the patient that he is going to give it a little push, and tell her not to worry if she hears a crack or pop; and then he would perform the thrust.

After manipulation, the osteopath will re-test the joint to ensure the technique has been effective, and will then do some gentle rhythmic traction to assist the recovery to normal movement. This will be followed by a little more articulation to use the increased movement gained from the thrust technique, after which the patient will be asked to sit up, to test the movement again.

At the end of the first treatment, the osteopath will propose a suitable interval until the next treatment.

The second session
On the patient's second visit, the osteopath would first of all enquire about the progress of her condition and its symptoms since the previous visit. Then he would repeat at least some of the initial examination process to ensure that the original diagnosis was still valid.

If she had suffered no adverse reaction, apart perhaps from a little stiffness, soreness or tiredness, and if the examination was consistent with expectations, the second treatment would be started. This would take a slightly different form from the first, because of changes found when examining her neck and shoulders, and would reflect the needs of the tissues at this time. On the other hand, if the reaction to the first treatment had been severe, for example if she had suffered a lot of discomfort, the osteopath would want to find out why this had occurred before repeating any movements. This would mean a thorough re-examination, to ensure that there had been no mistakes in the original assessment.

During the second treatment the osteopath would already

Exercise to help yourself Before attempting these exercises, please make sure that you are fit and healthy. Remember pain is a warning sign and should never be ignored!

Lumbar flexion Lie on your back with a pillow supporting your lower spine if you wish and gently raise both knees towards your chest. Clasp your hands around your knees and gently pull the knees down onto your stomach. Relax and repeat this exercise 10 times, breathing in as you pull down and out as you relax. This is a good exercise to flex the spine gently and open the spaces between the joints.

Standing sidebends Stand with your knees apart and gently try to run the palm of your hand down the outside of your leg. See how far you can reach without bending forward. Repeat for the other side again in sets of 10.

know the patient better and would probably be discussing general matters as well as the problem in hand. Hopefully, if she had been nervous on the first visit, she would be less so now. This would mean that the tissues would be more relaxed, too, which would allow him to perform slightly firmer treatment without producing any adverse reaction.

After the second treatment, the osteopath would probably give her more general advice regarding posture at work, and would check that she had been in touch with her opthalmologist to see about the eye test update.

The patient would probably also have a few questions to ask the osteopath, at this stage. Most osteopaths are only too pleased to answer such questions, because they show that the patient is taking an interest in the treatment. A good result is much more likely if the patient is interested in what is going on because this will also mean she is prepared to help herself.

It is at this stage that the osteopath might propose some simple exercises. These might consist of strengthening and mobilizing movements to optimize the effects of treatment.

Future treatment

If all goes according to plan, each visit the patient makes will be accompanied by reports of gradual improvement in range of movement, reduction of pain and general function. These improvements will be mirrored in the osteopath's examination process, which should reveal similar changes in the tissues to those felt by the patient herself. If the prognosis was reasonably accurate, she should have a substantial improvement after only a few visits, and further treatment beyond this should not be necessary.

In some cases, however, it is not possible to prevent recurrence of symptoms totally, because it is not possible for the patient to stop the activity that precipitated the problem. In the hypothetical case, the patient spends a great deal of time typing, and this inevitably sets up tension in the muscles of the neck and shoulders. In this case the osteopath would probably advise her to return for a general 'loosening' treatment after a period of three or four months. Depending on future progress, this interval might be further increased eventually.

Osteopathic treatment depends on many different factors, not least of which is the continuing feedback from both the patient, through questioning, and from their tissues, through examination.

Neck rolling Sit down comfortably and relax the shoulders. Now roll the neck and head round in a circle first one way and then the other but not too far back. Do not overdo this exercise, especially if you feel dizzy or faint. It is a good general mobility exercise for the neck and upper spine joints and muscles.

Water exercise Swimming or exercising in water is recommended for back or neck sufferers as the water buoys up the patient and helps carry the weight away from the spine. Breast stroke, if done gently and slowly, is probably better than freestyle because it involves less rotation of the trunk and more use of the long back muscles on each side working together.

CASE HISTORIES

LISA'S PREGNANCY

Lisa is a 32-year-old research assistant in a picture library. She is very active playing lots of squash and tennis, and is ten weeks' pregnant for the first time. She also has a bad back.

It started on the squash court when she twisted for an awkward ball. She felt a sharp pain straight away over her left buttock and had to stop. The pain got worse and by the time she was showered and dressed she could not drive home. She was frightened because she knew she was pregnant and thought that she had done something to harm the baby in some way. A friend drove her home and she phoned the doctor overseeing her pregnancy to request a home visit for that evening.

When Lisa's doctor examined her she told her not to worry and that her baby appeared fine. She diagnosed a pulled muscle and suggested bed rest for a few days. She explained that unfortunately because Lisa was pregnant she could not give her anything stronger than a paracetamol based analgesic for the pain. She did however suggest that Lisa use a hot-water bottle as heat often eased the pain in muscle cases.

She visited Lisa a couple of days later only to find that the pain, was, if anything, worse. Lying in bed was very difficult for any length of time, and turning over or getting up was very hard. Lisa suggested osteopathic manipulative therapy and the doctor thought this was a very good idea and suggested a practitioner qualified in this area.

When the osteopath came he took a careful case history of the pain and the way that the injury occurred. He examined Lisa standing and sitting and then laid her on her comfortable side to assess the range and quality of the spinal joints and pelvic joints. In this way he was able to ascertain what damage had been done and to which tissues.

He diagnosed a strain of the sacro-iliac joint on the left caused by the rotation force on the squash court, and made worse by the fact that during the pregnancy her ligaments are softened to allow the separation of the pelvic bones. He explained the problem and its treatment, and then started work straight away.

The first manipulation he did was with Lisa still on her side, using a gentle force to separate the bones of her sacro-iliac joint and allow the overlying muscles to relax. He used a very small HVT technique here with almost no leverage and a very small force. He then went on to move the other tissues in her buttock so as to allow the blood to flow in the deep muscles and ease the pain.

When Lisa saw the osteopath again she was much happier. Only a dull ache remained in her buttock and she was sleeping normally again. The osteopath explained that during her pregnancy her body posture would change to adapt to the growing baby, and this often causes back pain in the supporting muscles. He suggested Lisa make a monthly appointment during her pregnancy so that she could have treatment in advance of these postural changes. Also some of the other 'minor' side effects of pregnancy such as heartburn, leg cramps, and trapped nerves respond well too.

Lisa was delighted to be offered this sort of service and so she saw the osteopath throughout the pregnancy for this prophylactic care programme. Soon her back problem was a thing of the past.

A few weeks after the birth Lisa went back to the osteopath for her postnatal checkup. This is where the osteopath checks her pelvis for any problems. It is one of the few times in a patient's life where it is possible for a bone to be 'out of place'. He also checks the baby's head to make sure that the skull bones are moulding normally after the compression down the birth canal.

Lisa said that all was well except for the fact that the baby was not feeding easily. She felt uncomfortable feeding and the baby kept falling asleep on the breast and was soon hungry afterwards. This is a common problem he explained, and when he examined her he found that she had some lesions in her mid thoracic spine at brassiere strap level caused by the weight of her enlarged breasts dragging on the shoulder blades and supporting muscles. This was making her sitting position uncomfortable.

He corrected the lesions and worked on the deep muscles. He also suggested buying a special pillow which would support her better at this time. When Lisa phoned again she was feeling fine and her baby was feeding for longer and more fully. She also felt that her milk flow had improved.

And so Lisa was discharged happy and well. She felt that the preparation for delivery had helped her body cope with a time of increased hard work, and so made the whole process easier.

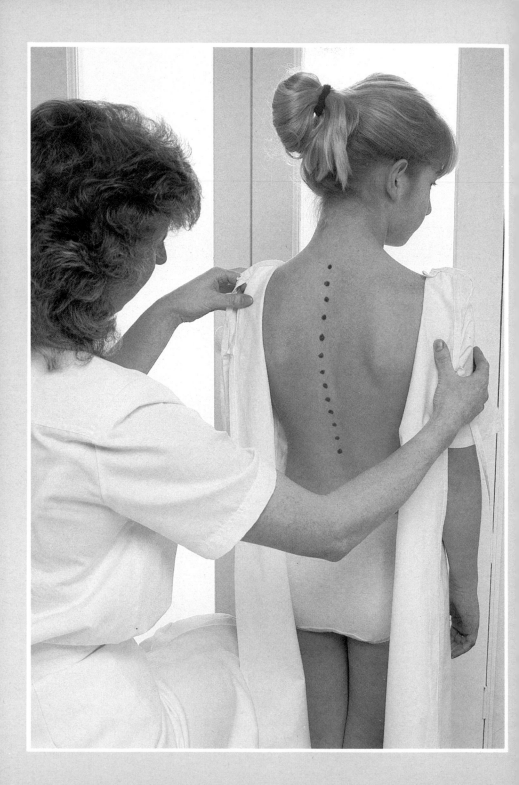

6

RELATED THERAPIES

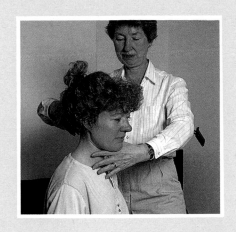

Once the nature and scope of osteopathy and osteopathic treatment are understood, it can be seen that there is only a superficial similarity between it and some of the methods used by other manipulative specialists. Some differentiation between these various methods is therefore useful. There has been much borrowing of methods from one discipline to another, and the divisions beween different manipulative therapies may, on first appearance, seem somewhat blurred. In fact, however, each has a distinct identity and a specific rationale and type of approach. There are even significant subdivisions within different approaches of manual treatment and therapies.

Osteopaths vary in their attitude to other manipulative therapies: some actively discourage patients from approaching such therapies, believing that it will detract from their osteopathic treatment; others work in close harmony with different holistic therapies; and some osteopaths themselves practise other therapies alongside osteopathy. In any case, it is sensible to learn something about other manipulative therapies and their possibilities, if only to eliminate them from your consideration.

There are good reasons for the multitude of different methods of alternative health care. Although practitioners of each discipline naturally tend to feel that their own is the best approach to any given problem, because of much better interdisciplinary dialogue in recent years, many of the best aspects of other holistic and related therapies have been combined by a number of health clinics. This can only be to the benefit of patients who can choose from a single or various complementary approaches.

As well as osteopaths, other professionals using manipulative measures as part of their work include chiropractors, some physiotherapists, manipulative physicians and surgeons, and some masseurs. In addition, practitioners of therapies such as acupressure, reflexology, rolfing, naturopathy and the Alexander technique also use touch in at least part of their treatment.

Although some practitioners use more than one therapy in their everyday practices, the thorough study and practice of any therapy to its highest levels requires a lifetime of application, and it is not possible to become fully adept at the whole range. The best compromise seems to be for a fully trained practitioner of one therapy (or at most two) also to know enough about the other approaches available to be able to recommend a different therapy if it would be more suitable for the patient.

How does a 'manipulation' performed by an osteopath differ from that performed by a member of one of the other manipulative professions? Despite a great many similarities, there are substantial differences in basic philosophy as well as in the actual techniques and the rationales that lie behind these techniques.

All medicine is either 'time-based' or 'touch-based'. The manipulative professions are obviously touch-based, and yet time comes into the equation as well. All touch-based therapy is powerful because of the human contact which is an essential part of these methods. Merely placing a hand on the body has a calming effect if it is done with suitable care. However, if all benefit was due only to that fact, touch alone would be sufficient. Sadly it is not. Each of the various therapies achieve beneficial results in different ways.

A comparison of all the therapies that utilize touch and manipulation is worthwhile, and each will be compared with osteopathy. While it is our intention to present a fair and balanced picture, inevitably the following summaries are written from an osteopath's point of view.

Chiropractic

Of all the para-medical professions using manipulation, modern chiropractic is probably the most similar to modern osteopathy.

The properly trained chiropractor is a specialist in the use of the hands to perform manipulative movements. Like osteopaths, chiropractors base their treatment on the premise that the health of the spine is vital to the health of the individual. They are also similar to osteopaths in their belief that the body contains or is able to manufacture everything necessary for its maintenance and repair.

It is not surprising that these similarities exist. The first chiropractor and the founder of the first school of chiropractic was an American by the name of Daniel David Palmer, a student of Andrew Taylor Still, the founder of osteopathy. Palmer disagreed with his teacher and is reported not to have finished his training with Still. Instead, he formed his own school, teaching a manipulative method that he was to call chiropractic.

Daniel David Palmer (1845-1913).

There are a number of differences between osteopathy and chiropractic, which are of both major and minor importance.

A chiropractor at work on her patient's shoulder. Chiropractic is based on the idea that mechanical disorders of the body are the result of specific local displacement of the spine.

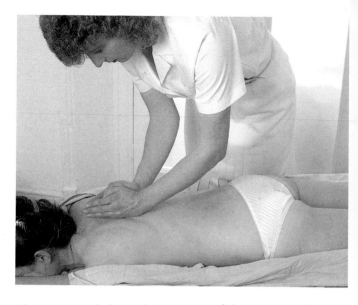

Chiropractors believe that sections of the spine can become displaced and need chiropractic manipulation to put them back into position. Osteopaths, on the other hand, believe that, while it is possible to have minor displacements, it is far more common to have a fixation, or jamming, without any real displacement. This locking, or limitation of movement, can be caused by a multitude of conditions.

Chiropractors use X-rays considerably more than osteopaths. The latter use them mainly to confirm what they have already discovered about a person's anatomy and to exclude the presence of disease. Chiropractors employ them primarily to diagnose badly aligned bones and to suggest which way to direct their corrective thrusts.

Both osteopaths and chiropractors are trained to consider the body as a whole. However, osteopaths tend to place much more emphasis on overall posture and on the mechanics of the bones and muscles, whereas chiropractors emphasize the very detailed local mechanics and tend to leave the overall situation to look after itself.

If an osteopath wishes to mobilize a spinal joint, he performs a variety of procedures prior to any manipulative thrust, if indeed this is necessary at all. A chiropractor traditionally produces a detailed diagnosis based on position and then performs a thrust in a certain direction to redirect the vertebrae into a specific position.

Another major difference between the two therapies is more practical, and concerns the technical procedures used. The actual manipulative thrusts performed by both sorts of therapists are fairly similar, as there is only a finite number of ways of manipulating the spine. The chief difference is that the osteopath is not normally governed by directions and pathways, but by the requirement to improve mobility. This frees him or her from the need to be quite so specific with regard to direction, which usually necessitates more force. Although not all chiropractic thrusts are forceful, as a general rule they will be more forceful than those given by osteopaths.

Chiropractors generally use a mechanical table, such as the Hi-Lo table, which has a multitude of adjustable elements and sprung sections. This allows them to use a variety of so-called 'recoil' thrust techniques. These are also used by osteopaths, but less frequently than techniques involving combined lever and thrust techniques.

Chiropractors often criticize osteopaths for being non-specific and using long-lever techniques; they maintain that chiropractic techniques are more accurate. Osteopaths counter this by stating that the way in which they soften up tissues before any manipulative thrust lessens the force that is necessary, and that lever techniques can be just as accurate, if not more so. In fact, the thoughtful, careful practitioner of either approach is equally effective in this respect.

The few reported cases of severe adverse reactions to manipulative measures relate primarily to ill-advised, or excessively forceful manipulation in the upper neck area. Chiropractic places great emphasis on this area as being responsible for many mechanical disturbances, and so many upper-neck manipulations are performed. Osteopaths feel that their particular approach, using mostly gentle procedures, is far less liable to cause problems in this quarter.

It is important to point out that, in the very few cases where problems have occurred, the chiropractic manipulations were performed by less than fully trained personnel – usually medically qualified doctors who had learned a few procedures on a postgraduate or weekend course. It is not possible to become an osteopath or a chiropractor after such a brief introduction to the subject.

The Chiropractic Advancement Association is a patient-oriented organization dedicated to furthering the political aims of chiropractic. In many countries, chiropractors outnumber osteopaths, and with vigorous campaigns of personal advertising and political lobbying have succeeded in gaining considerable ground. However, it must be said that in the UK, particularly with British-trained chiropractors, advertising and political activities are much more discreet. Indeed, the GCRO and the British Chiropractors Association (BCA) are working together on lobbying the government for registration and regulation of the manipulative therapies.

Manipulative physiotherapy

Many physiotherapists use manipulative methods as part of their work. Traditionally, their training is fairly broad based, and during it practitioners learn which techniques interest them and choose to specialize later by joining a postgraduate society and undertaking further training.

Not many of us visiting a hospital physiotherapy department will be treated to such costly therapy as this deep heat treatment, being administered to a football hero. Such treatment is designed to prevent pain and stiffness in the limbs due to the exacerbation of old injuries.

In the UK, the organization that trains and looks after the interests of physiotherapists concerned with manipulation is the Manipulative Association of Chartered Physiotherapists (MACP). The MACP extends membership only to fully-qualified physiotherapists and then only after a designated period after qualification. To become fully-accredited members, physiotherapists must attend a series of part-time courses and a full-time course lasting three months. After passing a

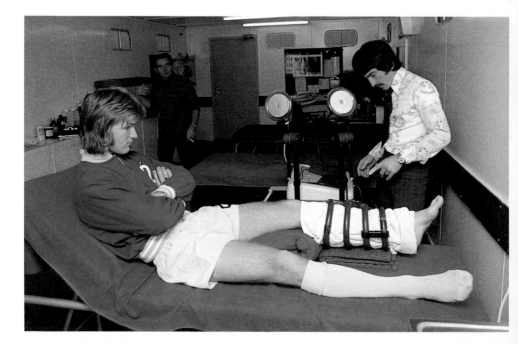

final examination, the physiotherapist is elected to full membership.

Until very recently, physiotherapy training did not include medical diagnosis. Physiotherapists were trained to carry out a range of procedures on the specific instructions of a doctor and they were not allowed to treat a patient without a doctor's referral. Those using manipulative measures were careful to use the word 'assessment' rather than 'diagnosis'. Their treatment was strictly controlled, and consisted of exercise therapy, electrotherapy and some massage.

This situation has changed markedly in recent years. Physiotherapy training schools have, in many cases, developed degree courses – including, to a limited extent, training in manipulative treatment – and the profession as a whole has become more assertive. Members of the medical profession have admitted that they really did not know the full scope and nature of the physiotherapy, and its practitioners have gradually been given much more autonomy. In addition, increasing numbers of practitioners have taken up private practice.

The actual difference in the approach used by physiotherapists from that used by osteopaths hinges once again on theory and technique.

The physiotherapist believes in the presence of a 'somatic dysfunction' (mechanical disorder) in the same way as the osteopath. However, the significance of such dysfunction to the general well-being of the patient is not considered as important by the physiotherapist as it is by the osteopath. As for the actual techniques used by the two professions, there is only a finite number of manual forms available, and to the untrained eye it is often difficult to see any difference between them.

Osteopathic manipulative treatment is an art based on a science, which has evolved over many years. There have been major contributions from particularly skilled or gifted members of the profession, but the basic methods have remained much as they were at the outset, although they have become more refined.

There have been two major influences on physiotherapeutic technique: the teaching of the English doctor James Cyriax and the Australian Geoffrey Maitland.

Dr Cyriax, a medically qualified manipulator, wrote several books on diagnosis and therapeutic procedures of manual medicine. In particular, his diagnostic methods have been widely acclaimed and, indeed, are taught to all physiotherapists learning manual techniques. These methods form the science of his approach. On the other hand, the actual technical procedures he advocated were often very violent, and were based on the theory that all spinal problems are due to minute disc displacements and that vigorous manipulation is necessary to put these right. When he was shown gentle osteopathic manipulation based on a delicate, educated touch, however, Cyriax felt that they could not be learned in the time available to most physiotherapists.

Cyriax's approach was taken up by many physiotherapists. This was probably because of his strong personality, and the paucity of other available methods. Unfortunately, his extreme antagonism toward those he called 'lay manipulators' – in which category he included osteopaths and chiropractors – was instilled in many of his students. In the later years of his life, however, Cyriax did come to admit that the fully-trained and registered osteopath was in possession of an effective, safe and useful therapy.

Geoffrey Maitland, an Australian physiotherapy teacher, has written several books on manipulation. He categorized the various manipulative approaches used by physiotherapists, and put them in a form which was simple to communicate to students. Most of the teaching done by the MACP today is based on his categories of technique.

He objects to people referring to the 'Maitland method', but inevitably this has happened. His approach emphasizes safety at all times, the use of gradually increasing amounts of force, and constant feedback from the patient, as well as re-examination by the practitioner.

Admirable though these principles are, a problem has arisen: the 'art' of the manipulative skill has been discarded in favour of a set of specific rules that are slavishly followed. In addition, Maitland manipulation has come out badly in several trials in which it was compared with rest, the wearing of corsets and placebo therapy.

Many osteopaths would argue that manipulation as practised by physiotherapists (influenced by Maitland) has lost much of its art in the endeavour to make it more scientific. Osteopaths use manipulative methods as part of their approach to whole-patient care. In contrast to physiotherapy, osteopathy seeks to treat the whole patient, rather than concentrating almost entirely on the bodily system that presents the most obvious symptoms.

When a physiotherapist wishes to enrol at a school of osteopathy, he or she is only allowed a minimum reduction in required classes because of previous training. Some physiotherapists feel that this is unfair, maintaining that much of the training is duplicated. However, experience has shown that physiotherapy training in many subjects is not as thorough as that given at schools of osteopathy and it has been found necessary to keep study reductions to a minimum because postgraduate physiotherapists could not keep up with undergraduate osteopaths unless they had done the full course.

There have been some moves in the world of physiotherapy to introduce some principles which could be said to be almost osteopathic. There has been much discussion between the two professions, and many things that osteopaths have been saying and doing for years are being taken up by some physiotherapists.

There are three reasons for this. First, truth is self-evident, and with sufficient study, it is obvious that much of what has been said in osteopathic literature is obviously true. Second, many more physiotherapists are going into private practice. The requirements of the commercial world are such that it is essential that the best practitioners keep up with the competition. Third, increasing numbers of physiotherapists, particularly the private practitioners, need to make diagnoses, and prescribe their own treatment. Until fairly recently, osteopaths and chiropractors have been the only manipulative practitioners doing this, so it is natural that physiotherapists will adopt some of their methods.

Today, there is probably far less distrust between the two professions than ever before. Much useful dialogue has gone on, and natural demarcation between cases that each different discipline can handle best is progressively taking place. In fact, most registered osteopaths refer patients to chartered physiotherapists when they consider such treatment is appropriate. Increasingly, the converse is also true.

The appellation 'physiotherapist' is not protected by law and, in the same way that anyone can call themselves an osteopath, a chiropractor or a manipulative specialist, anyone can call themselves a physiotherapist. However, in the UK prospective patients can contact the physiotherapists' regulatory body (the Chartered Society of Physiotherapists) for the name of a fully qualified physiotherapist. In the United States, patients can contact the American Physical Therapy Association for the same for the same information.

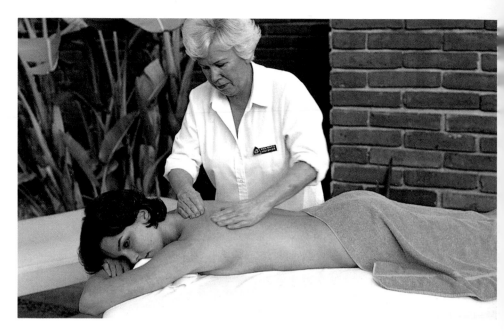

Massage is probably the oldest touch therapy in the world, and there are many varieties to choose from. Unlike osteopathy, general, non specific massage is time-based: the masseur continues until relaxation is achieved. This is fine if your problem is merely tiredness or stiffness after a tough workout, but will not help any more serious complaints.

Massage

Another form of therapy which has been bedevilled by variations in training and qualifications is therapeutic massage. As with osteopaths, chiropractors and physiotherapists, anyone can call themselves a masseur or masseuse, and offer to treat people by any of a variety of forms of massage.

Apart from a limited number of unsavoury establishments offering massage euphemistically, which have done much damage to serious practitioners, there is a wide variety of genuine types of massage, mostly with a broadly therapeutic aim. Massage itself is one of the oldest forms of physical therapy, with evidence of practice throughout the history of Middle Eastern, Mediterranean and Oriental and Asian civilizations.

Nowadays, many masseurs become interested in massage through their involvement in sports. They become sports masseurs or 'trainers' and, when they find that they have a natural flair for manual therapy, even call themselves osteopaths. There are ethical organizations teaching massage, whose advanced courses include joint manipulation. Most of their members do not call themselves osteopaths, but because of increasing pressure from the public for osteopathic treatment, some do.

Joint-manipulation courses are of necessity somewhat superficial compared to the full time courses of osteopathy, certainly in a medical training sense. They are primarily concerned with pain syndromes, and not the general approach to osteopathic medicine.

Physicians and surgeons

Many physicians use a few manipulative techniques for specific syndromes such as stiff necks or lower back pain. They would not call themselves osteopaths, and many of them know little about osteopathy other than what they have been told by their patients. They have often learned manipulative techniques from a book, or have attended specifically designed weekend courses.

In the early 1960s an organization was formed in Britain, called the British Association of Manipulative Medicine (BAMM). One of the founder members of BAMM was James Cyriax, the influential innovator in the world of physiotherapy. His particularly forceful methods dominated the association for some time, although increasingly, the work of medically-qualified osteopaths was seen to be more gentle and no less effective.

There are a number of medically-qualified osteopaths in Britain. Most have studied medicine first, and then have studied the shortened course at the London College of Osteopathic Medicine (LCOM) or the British School of Osteopathy. There are a few medically trained osteopaths who qualified first in osteopathy and then went on to study medicine. This is, however, a very long route. The medically-qualified osteopaths by no means dominate the BAMM, but have amply demonstrated the quality of osteopathic methods. In the USA, the situation is different (see Chapter 7).

Most members of BAMM readily admit that they practice manipulation as a 'hobby'. They are attracted to the quick results it achieves and the challenge of the skills required. Many of them have only had the benefit of a very few short courses, and are inevitably able to use only a limited range of techniques. Most manipulative physicians use their techniques as 'tools' added to their gamut of other methods, rather than as part of an overall approach to patient care.

The range of skills between the most experienced and expert and the least expert is very varied. Of course, they are all qualified doctors and have a deep understanding of the nature of disease and the necessity for caution in some of their manoeuvres. However, limited experience often results in limited effectiveness, and as a substitute for this, high levels of force are sometimes employed. This is far from desirable for reasons of both safety and comfort.

Quite a large number of orthopaedic surgeons use some manipulation as part of their work. This is generally directed toward the replacement of dislocations, and to breaking down adhesions – neither requirement falls within the scope of osteopathy. These movements are usually performed when patients are under anaesthetic – and these practitioners admit that such manipulation would be too painful for a conscious patient. In stark contrast, anaesthesia does not form part of the everyday work of osteopaths; osteopathic techniques are rarely so painful or forceful as to require it.

The osteopath's point of view is, emphatically, that performing a few manipulations is not the same thing as carrying out osteopathic treatment. Most manipulative surgeons do not use the full range of techniques employed by osteopaths. They concentrate instead on the short sharp thrust procedures. Osteopaths feel that, valuable as these are, they should only form a part of the overall approach to the patient if the practitioner is going to use manual methods.

Although many orthopaedic surgeons use some manipulative techniques in their work, the bulk of their expertise covers joint replacement and fracture repair. Here an orthopaedic surgeon examines a prosthetic hip and thigh/leg assembly, comparing it to the original model it is to replace.

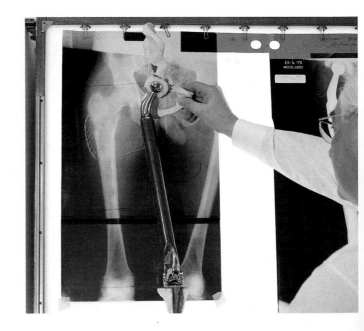

Other therapies

There are several other therapies whose techniques superficially relate to the work of osteopaths. There are also various types of 'body work' therapies, which also bear a passing resemblance to osteopathy, but none of them has a similar regulatory organization responsible for training, registration and professional control of practitioners. These therapists do not act as full primary-care practitioners.

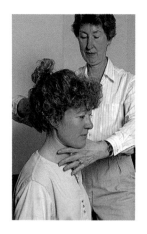

Acupressure bears some relation to acupuncture. Practitioners use manipulations of trigger points on the surface of the body to treat disorders throughout the body. It is actually a massage technique, *Shiatsu*, centred on acupuncture points and meridians.

The Alexander Technique a method of correcting postural imbalance, was invented by an Australian actor, F. Matthias Alexander in the late nineteenth century. It seeks to re-educate the body and thereby improve mental and physical health. Teachers of the Technique train for a period of three to four years. Lessons are given either in group classes or as individual tuition and pupils undertake a series of about 30 sessions. The Alexander Technique may be used to help relieve such conditions as asthma, back pain, neuralgia, digestive problems and migraine, and it helps combat the effects of stress.

The Alexander Technique is a method of gentle guidance to correct postural imbalances and re-educate the body to better health.

Naturopathy is a therapy that very easily complements the work of osteopathy. Indeed, there are some osteopaths who are also practising naturopaths. Naturopathy sees disease as a consequence of a build-up of toxins in the body from bad diet, inadequate exercise and excessive stress. Naturopathy uses fasting, diet, exercise and massage to return the body to a state in which it may begin to rid itself of illness.

Reflexology is also called 'zone therapy'. This therapy uses massage and manipulation of points on the feet and hands to treat conditions in the rest of the body.

Rolfing is a type of deep massage in which the hands work on the fascia (the elastic tissue between the muscles and under the skin) and the muscles to stretch and remodel the body so that it becomes closer to an idea of what is 'normal'. It has a few similarities with osteopathy and its founder, Ida Rolf, had some osteopathic training.

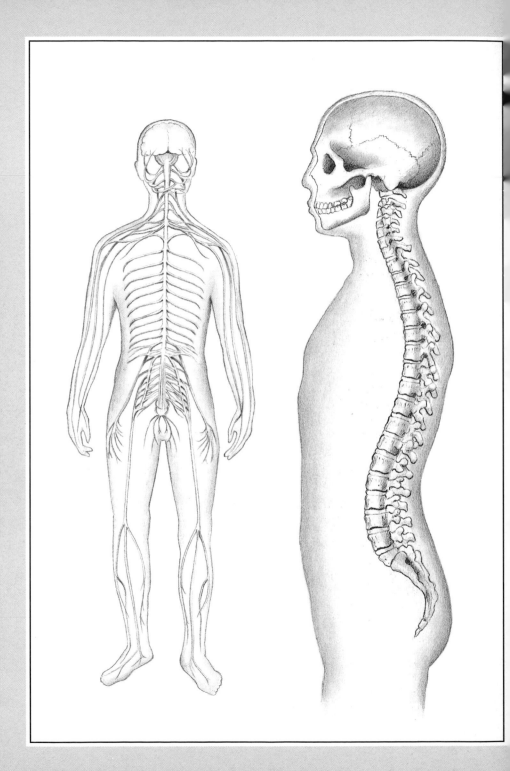

7

FOUNDATIONS
OF OSTEOPATHY

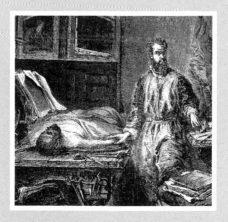

Since before the birth of Hippocrates (called 'the father of medicine') two thousand years ago, there has been argument and discussion among those who see themselves as healers about the relative importance of the patient on the one hand or the illness on the other. Today this argument is still not settled, with one school of thought looking at the factors outside the body that cause disease, and the other school looking at the disease process itself as the reason for ill health.

Medicine's great debate

In ancient Greece there were also two conflicting points of view. One was the Hippocratic school, based at the island of Kos, and the other, called the Cnidian school, was based at Cnidus in Asia Minor. The Hippocratic school maintained that diseases arose from natural causes. They were not afflictions rained on the heads of wayward mortals by angry or jealous gods, but nature's way of dealing with an ever variable state somewhere between good and bad health. Hippocrates thought that physicians could aid nature and thus restore their patients to good health.

The Cnidian school of thought was based on a diametrically opposed philosophy. It maintained that the disease process itself needed to be hunted and destroyed in order to have good health. And whereas the Hippocratic school thought that the factors that caused disease were essentially external, the Cnidian school regarded them as being internal.

Osteopathy is a holistic science. It views health and ill health in terms of the whole body. Osteopaths are firm advocates of the Hippocratic way because they feel that mankind is a product of the environment, and that changing the environment – be it postural, emotional or physical – encourages better health by removing or modifying those factors that predispose or promote disease.

The development of medicine

From these earliest beginnings made by the ancient Greeks, Western medicine underwent little change for the next thousand years. Other cultures and civilizations in the Far East and Middle East were developing their healing systems too, and strange as it may seem they were not far away from the arguments that were taking place in the West. The theory and philosophy of acupuncture, originating in China, again recognizes internal and external forces in relation to disorders, as does the Ayurvedic system of healing in India.

In the Middle Ages, European medicine was in a state of decline. Magic and mysticism were bound up with the healing arts, as demonstrated by the following cure for epilepsy from the sixth century.

Take a nail from a wrecked ship, make it into a bracelet and set therein the bone from the heart of a stag taken from its body while alive. Put it on the left arm; you will be astonished at the result.

'The Story of Medicine' by Kathy and Mike Eldon

The Church became involved too, with disease being seen as God's revenge for man's sin and iniquity, an idea not so far removed from those of the ancient Greeks or even tribal superstitions among primitive peoples. If you became ill it was because your mortal soul was in danger, and purges and cathartics were used to drive the evil spirits from the body. The mentally ill were locked in chains or in hospitals like Bedlam in London – themselves little better than prisons –

The gin-sodden protagonist of William Hogarth's Rake's Progress ended up in Bedlam, the London madhouse. The inmates of such establishments were seen as a sort of beguiling cabaret by the rest of 18th-century society.

A major breakthrough in medicine was made by William Harvey (1578-1657) who discovered the fact that blood circulated round the body. He was court physician first to James I and then Charles I, to whom he is shown expounding his theory, using a deer as a demonstration model.

where people would pay to look at the wretched inmates as a source of sport.

Surgery was in its infancy and often consisted of little more than amputation followed by hot pitch applied to the stump to cauterize and seal the wound. If you did not die from a wound infection, the shock of the operation performed when you were conscious – or at best 'anaesthetized' with rum – would probably kill you. The army surgeons were the most experienced at dealing with wounds simply because they saw so many of them. The family physician had blood letting as his mainstay of treatment, which worked or not according to the circumstances. It was really a matter of chance whether you died or got better. Indeed, if the latter, it was probably in spite of the treatment rather than because of it.

Sixteenth-century discoveries

A series of revolutionary discoveries made between the mid-sixteenth century and the early eighteenth century were

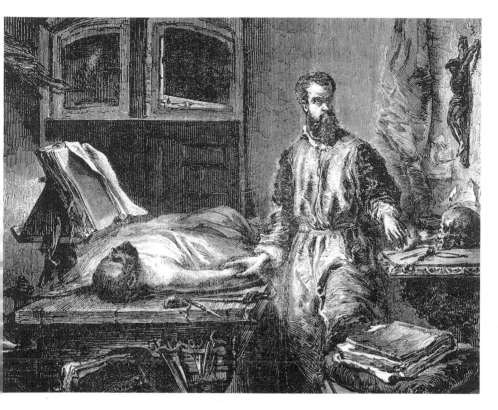

to change the way doctors thought about disease. Many of Hippocratic medicine's basic tenets were to be challenged and attacked.

Vesalius, the anatomist, published a work in 1543 that described the human body in far greater detail than had ever before been attempted. In a public lecture in 1616, William Harvey demonstrated a model of the human circulation that reflected the system science describes today. He dispelled the theories of flux and humours, which people thought were responsible for the movement of body fluids.

Thomas Sydenham (1624–1689), thought by many to be the founder of modern clinical medicine, brought his remarkable observational skills to the hospital wards with the words 'Young man, go to the bedside, there alone can you learn about disease!' Sydenham was a clinician first and foremost, and he firmly believed that we must study our patients if we want to find out why they are sick. He rejected dogma, and firmly and clearly observed all aspects of disease,

Andreas Vesalius (1514-1564) the Belgian anatomist whose great work De Humani Corporis Fabrica *(On the fabric of the human body) earned him the death sentence from the Spanish Inquisition for bodysnatching and dissection. Vesalius had described with great accuracy and many precise illustrations the biology of the human skeleton and nervous system, thus ushering medical science into the modern age.*

carefully recording what he saw. His observations were accurate and concise, and for many years formed the basis of clinical case teaching. He recognized fever and inflammation as the body's attempt to rid itself of disease. He even looked at diet and hygiene in an attempt to discover why chronic disease took hold. Remarkably, all of this took place some two hundred years before Lister and Pasteur.

Andrew Taylor Still, the father of osteopathy

The American physician Andrew Taylor Still was an unusual man from an unusual background. History relates that his great-grandfather was tomahawked and scalped by Chief Black Wolf of the Shawnees in 1786. His father, Abram Still, was a physician and a Methodist minister. Andrew was born on 6 August 1828 at Jonesborough, Lee County, Virginia.

From an early age, we are told, young Andrew showed an interest in following in his father's footsteps rather than in spending his time working on the family farm. His father was keen to encourage him but he also wanted the boy to have the best education possible.

There were two routes to medicine in the United States in the late nineteenth century. One involved becoming a student attending a medical school and paying fees to learn from the master surgeons and physicians after formal classes in anatomy and diagnosis. The other was for the prospective student to find a doctor who would take him on as an apprentice.

Still had the best of both worlds. He was able to study at the College of Physicians and Surgeons in Kansas City, where he eventually graduated, while at the same time he was able to follow his father on his rounds and learn from the way he treated his patients. In this way Andrew started to practise medicine in the state of Missouri, where he obtained his state licence.

Medicine in the 1800s

Like everything else in frontier America in the last half of the nineteenth century, medicine was rough, tough and primitive.

Anaesthetics were not introduced into surgical practice until the 1860s, even though the painkilling properties of chloroform and ether were well known. There was fierce religious opposition to employing them because it was felt by some that the use of anaesthetics was sacrilegious and that pain was given by God and therefore inviolate.

There was also the different danger of overusing these

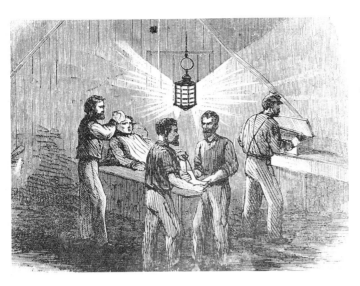

Hot surgery on the battlefields of the American Civil War may not have been much fun for the soldiers, who were not always given anaesthetics, but it taught the doctors a great deal about human anatomy. Andrew Taylor Still served as a surgeon in the Union Army.

strong agents. Surgeons operating on patients who could not feel the pain also had more time to work, so frequently became overzealous, often cutting away far more tissue than was necessary. Patients also become addicted to the strong opiates and other drugs used, and this in turn created more problems for the doctor to deal with.

Operating rooms were filthy places with little more than sawdust on the floor to soak up the blood and body fluids. Surgeons operated in aprons or frock coats, not seeing any need to wash between cases and not even wearing gloves. It was not until 1865 that Joseph Lister insisted on spraying the delivery room in his hospital with a solution of chlorinated lime. He also insisted on his colleagues washing their hands in the lime solution too. At first they were so offended by his effrontery that they threw him out of the hospital and tried to turn him into a laughing stock.

Pharmacology was likewise in its infancy and highly dangerous. The toxic mercury compound calomel was a standard preparation in both hospital and general practice, and the dosage varied from practitioner to practitioner. A broad herbal pharmacopoeia was in use, with again many variations as regards to potency and prescription. Each practitioner had his own favourites. Some were excellent and went on to form the basis of modern drug therapies, such as dried foxglove (which contains digitalis) used for treating heart ailments. Others fell by the wayside as medical science progressed.

The tragedy of 1874 and afterwards

In this climate of medical ignorance came an event of enormous magnitude in the life of Dr Still. In 1874 Missouri was stricken by an epidemic of what we now understand to be viral meningitis. Dr Still lost three children that spring because he had no way to cure them. He was a doctor, a skilled and trained physician, and yet his training was useless when it came to saving the lives of his own family.

Still emerged from this tragedy with a renewed passion to discover the reasons why some people became sick, and why others were spared. He grew to despise and reject the system of medicine that produced doctors who were content to amputate limbs incautiously and overuse drugs in an attempt to provide relief.

He began to feel that his whole approach to medicine was wrong, and for the next ten years he searched for a new concept, a new idea based on his beloved anatomy. His religious background led him to the belief that man was created in God's image. With this in mind he surmised that, if this was the case, at the point of creation all must have been correct, and anything that happened to the body to produce disease was a result of an alteration of this basic fact. In other words, it was an alteration in the structure of man that caused an alteration in the function.

This simple step led him on to the path of creating his new concept of the nature of health and illness. He regarded the skeleton as more than simply the physical framework on which muscles are hung, rather as an organizer of normal functioning life. Not only are all muscles attached to the skeleton, it also provides a protective framework for the brain and spinal cord (the skull and spine) and for the vital organs (the ribs). Therefore any alteration in the structure of the skeletal system and its attendant muscles will affect the function of the organs it serves. He called this new system of medicine osteopathy (*osteon* is Greek for bone), because it was based on the bony framework.

Dr Still was convinced that the answer to disease lay within the patient. If you can prevent someone from becoming sick in the first place, then surely this must be better than curing them after the event.

This is how osteopathy began. It is taught today, more than a hundred years later, with the same set of principles in mind, modified only slightly to bring it up to date with new discoveries.

Osteopathy in the United States

Dr Still was a doctor first and foremost – a dissatisfied doctor certainly, but a doctor nevertheless. He was dissatisfied with medical practice in the latter half of the nineteenth century and so he set out to reform it.

Osteopathy today in the United States is known as osteopathic medicine. Americans are encouraged to call their practitioners Doctor and to refer to them as their osteopathic physician (rather than their osteopath). A Doctor of Osteopathy (DO) is recognized in every state in the Union as an equal to a Medical Doctor (MD). DOs serve with equal rights in the armed forces, and in the prison and social services.

Osteopathic medicine is different from orthodox or conventional medicine because the patient with the disease is considered more important than the disease itself. OMT (osteopathic manipulative therapy) is taught as part of the undergraduate training and is regarded as an adjunct to other therapies such as surgery or drugs. The training programmes of the MD and DO are almost identical, with the exception of OMT and the importance placed by osteopathic physicians on the reason behind the disease.

Class of 1893. The original graduating class of the American School of Osteopathy, Kirksville, Missouri, surrounding its mentor, Dr Andrew Taylor Still. The class consisted of 17 men, 5 women and a skeleton named Columbus.

John Martin Littlejohn John Martin Littlejohn was born in Glasgow in 1865. He was a highly intelligent man of letters obtaining an MA in 1889, a divinity degree BD in 1890 and a law degree LLB in 1892. He also studied anatomy and physiology at Kelvin Hall in Glasgow and in 1889 was awarded the William Hunter Gold Medal in Forensic Medicine.

In 1892, he emigrated to the USA for health reasons and in 1897 he consulted Dr Still for a throat condition. Still's treatment so impressed him that he resolved to study under Still at Kirksville. Because of his experience in physiology, he was invited to give lectures in the subject and was later made Dean of the Faculty under Still as President.

Littlejohn graduated and gained his diploma from Kirksville in 1900 and went on to found the second school of osteopathy in Chicago, which he called the American College of Osteopathic Medicine and Surgery. He eventually returned to England to found the British School of Osteopathy in London. Today the school bears his name, as the building in Suffolk Street that houses the present day BSO is called Littlejohn House.

It is because of this bias in teaching that more than 75 per cent of all graduates from osteopathic teaching hospitals ultimately work in general practice. In allopathic medicine, more than 75 per cent of graduates hope eventually to specialize.

This summarizes the situation in theory as it applies in the United States. However, in practice the picture is a little different. It is certainly the case that many DOs each year go into general practice, but it is fast becoming the norm that after a few years a DO and an allopathic MD are virtually indistinguishable. The identity of osteopathy in the United States seems to be under threat from assimilation with allopathy, apart from one or two notable centres where the struggle to retain the difference goes on.

William Garner Sutherland

One of the people whose teachings inspire the purists among American osteopaths is Dr William Sutherland, the father of the cranio-sacral technique (see pp. 110–111). Dr Sutherland was a student of Still's at Kirksville in 1895. His studies led him to conclude that the sutures (joins) where the skull bones meet were important. He spent 30 years developing his conclusion into a diagnostic and treatment programme.

Osteopathy in Britain

Osteopathy arrived in Britain in 1903. The first practitioners were American DOs looking for new places to practise. In 1911 the British Osteopathic Association was formed, with membership confined to graduates of the American schools.

These first pioneers were regarded as quacks by the British medical establishment. Only rarely, however, did they come into contact with them. By and large they were left alone to practise as they wished as long as they did no harm.

The first event of any real significance was the return to Britain of Dr John Martin Littlejohn in 1913. He was the first to develop plans and ideas for the establishment of a British School of Osteopathy. John Littlejohn was born in Glasgow in 1865. An academic and a scholar, he studied at Glasgow University and obtained his MA in 1869, a BD in 1890, and a law degree (LLB) in 1892.

In 1892 for health reasons he emigrated to the United States, and in 1897 he consulted Dr Still at Kirksville for a throat infection. Littlejohn was so impressed with Still's practice and philosophy that he decided to stay and study under him.

Littlejohn's contribution to osteopathy while in the United States was the addition of physiology to the anatomy so loved by Dr Still. He was invited to give lectures in physiology while still a student, eventually being appointed Dean of the faculty of Physiology with Dr Still as President. Littlejohn graduated in 1900 and went on to found the second school of osteopathy at Chicago, the American College of Osteopathic Medicine and Surgery.

The British School of Osteopathy

On 7 March 1917, the British School of Osteopathy (BSO) was incorporated in London. It was first located in Vincent Square, then in Abbey House in Victoria Street. In the first few years Dr Littlejohn and his small staff were responsible for the teaching, using a syllabus based on the American system. In 1980 a decision was taken to undergo a major programme of expansion and so new premises were taken at 1–4 Suffolk Street just off Trafalgar Square.

In honour of the founding father of British osteopathy the spacious new building was named Littlejohn House. This building now houses a school of some 400 students and more than 100 trained staff. The course involves four years of full-time study, and the school incorporates a clinic that is currently treating more than 1,000 patients each week. The patron of the school is the Princess Royal HRH The Princess Anne. All this has grown from quite humble beginnings more than 70 years ago.

HRH The Princess Royal, Patron of the British School of Osteopathy.

The fight for legislation in Britain

From the earliest days in Britain, DOs have sought recognition by Parliament for their work and practice. Under common law, anybody who wants to can call himself (or herself) an osteopath because there is no legal requirement for training of any kind. There is no legislation to protect either the profession or the public from charlatans who seek to use osteopathy for their own ends. In 1931, 1933 and 1934 bills to regulate the practice of osteopathy were submitted to the House of Commons, but the bills were not debated.

In 1935 there was a select committee of the House of Lords whose aim was once again to investigate osteopathy with a view to legislation. This committee was to prove an unmitigated disaster for the osteopathic profession for many reasons. The opponents of the bill were members of the orthodox medical establishment of the day, including the

British Medical Association and the Royal College of Physicians and Surgeons. In contrast the supporters of the bill were the British Osteopathic Association (the British branch of the AOA), and the fledgling British School of Osteopathy. Dr Littlejohn was unhappy about the whole affair but was persuaded – against his better judgement – to proceed. When he was produced as a witness he was subjected to a cruel and bitter personal attack. His response was to withdraw and remain largely silent. When he did speak he was hesitant and often philosophical rather than forthright and practical.

The report of the committee after several months' deliberation was damning in the extreme. It maintained that the only existing establishment for training osteopaths in Britain was 'of negligible importance, inefficient for its purpose and in thoroughly dishonest hands'!

Littlejohn was stunned by this attack and some say he never fully recovered from it. The door to legal recognition was slammed shut and was to remain closed for the next 50 years.

The only thing of value to come from the whole affair was a recommendation from the Minister of Health that the osteopaths themselves set up a voluntary register of properly trained persons so that the public would be able to distinguish between the untrained osteopath and the practitioner who had completed at least some form of training. This was duly accepted and the next year on 22 July 1936 The General Council and Register of Osteopaths (GCRO) was incorporated as a limited company. The articles of association permitted full membership to American DOs and to graduates of the British School of Osteopathy.

1930 to the present day
From the 1930s until the 1980s, the school carried on training students who graduated with their diploma in osteopathy, the DO. The training was musculo-skeletal based. The principles of osteopathy laid down by Dr Still have always been adhered to in Britain, but British osteopaths have never attempted to call themselves practitioners of an alternative form of medicine, as have their American counterparts. Likewise they do not practise obstetrics or surgery nor does their training involve any course in pharmacology or drug prescription.

Instead British osteopaths have developed and refined the manual skills first laid down by Doctor Still, both in diagnosis and treatment. They have continued to specialize in the same OMT from which the American Colleges have turned away.

Osteopathy elsewhere in Europe

There are many part-time schools of osteopathy throughout Europe, particularly in France and Belgium. In France osteopaths have formed the Fédération des Osteopaths de France (FOF) and in Belgium the Société des Osteopaths Belge (SBO). Before attending classes in these schools, students must be trained physiotherapists. They then spend four or five years at weekend seminars learning osteopathic diagnosis, principles, and techniques before presenting themselves for examination. They are examined theoretically and practically by internal and external examiners and if they pass they are awarded the Certificate of Osteopathy (CO). They then spend the next two years preparing a thesis before the diploma examination and are awarded the DO certificate.

The practice of osteopathic medicine is still not legally recognized in France but circumstances are changing, and the future holds promise for the thousands of practitioners throughout Europe who have been under legal persecution for wanting to practise this form of therapy.

In Spain, the same situation applies, but Spanish graduates from the British School of Osteopathy living in Bilbao have plans to open an osteopathic medical centre and school of osteopathy there as soon as the time is right.

Osteopathy in Australia

Australia has a long history of association with British-trained graduates who have settled in the country, mainly around Melbourne in the state of Victoria. From 1987 there has been a programme run by the Philip Institute in Melbourne which is based on the course run at the British School of Osteopathy. Thus before long Australians will start to graduate their own home-trained graduates and set up their own register of practitioners.

The future

The future of osteopathy in Britain lies in the ability of the GCRO as the major osteopathic organization to unite all of the osteopathic schools under one umbrella and to lobby for legislation. (The government is sympathetic.) The BSO is applying to have its programme validated by the Council for National Academic Awards as a BSc degree in osteopathic studies. Consequently the future looks good in Britain, with more than 200 graduates each year qualifying from the four Register-approved schools.

8

FINDING
AND CONSULTING
AN OSTEOPATH

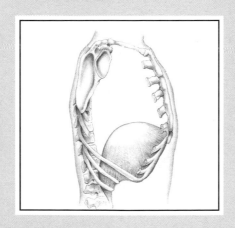

Finding an osteopath is rather easier in the USA than the rest of the world, but the terminology is rather different.

In other countries, manual practitioners who follow the teachings of Andrew Taylor Still call themselves osteopaths, but in the USA there was a move to dissociate the profession from a cultist approach to health and to let the public know that osteopathic medicine was 'normal' and nothing 'freaky'. The result is that now osteopathy the science has become known as 'osteopathic medicine' and its practitioners 'osteopathic physicians and surgeons'. In the USA the DO stands for doctor of osteopathy and the graduates of the osteopathic schools are encouraged to use the title 'Doctor'. This is in direct distinction to the practitioners who operate in the rest of the world, whose DO signifies diplomate in osteopathy and who call themselves 'osteopaths'. In the USA the osteopathic doctors have equal status with their MD colleagues in every way. They can work in all hospitals competing equally for jobs, as well as working in the armed forces and in government service.

Today there are more than 20,000 licensed DOs practising in 50 states and in the District of Columbia. Because the emphasis of osteopathic education is on primary health care, many DOs have a strong commitment to general practice and family based medicine. Approximately 75 per cent of graduating DOs become family doctors and over a half of them practise in rural areas.

Before the turn of the century, some of the original osteopaths shunned their colleagues who wanted to practise a wide view of medicine encompassing surgery and obstetrics. They maintained that illness was only approachable via the lesions in the musculoskeletal system. It was the great Doctor Still himself who entered the debate in 1901 when he insisted that students at Kirksville were to be taught the operative surgery commonly performed in rural areas and that they were to become proficient in the handling of obstetric cases.

The first advisory board for specialities in osteopathic hospitals was established in 1939 with a speciality in radiology. A full range of speciality training now exists in every field of human medicine from nuclear medicine to obstetrics, from psychiatry to paediatrics, from orthopaedics, to dermatology with internships and residency programs in osteopathic hospitals all over the country. Following the completion of the residency programs and the passing of the board exams, the DO can become a specialist in his own right.

Osteopathic training

Osteopathic medical education (both graduate and under-graduate) is provided by the colleges of osteopathic medicine. All of the colleges are accredited by the AOA.

Admission to the colleges requires a minimum of three years of pre-professional education in a college or university course. Some colleges require a BA. All osteopathic colleges require students to have passed the Medical College Admission Test.

An entering student must have credit for at least six semester hours in English with 12 hours recommended, six to eight semester hours in organic and inorganic chemistry, physics and biology, and elective courses reflecting a broad cultural background.

Once students start at an osteopathic college, they will study for four academic years. Subjects will include anatomy, physiology, biochemistry, pharmacology, pathology, micro-biology, paediatrics, obstetrics, gynaecology, surgery, psychiatry, neurology, physical diagnosis etc – in other words, all the subjects you would expect student doctors to study.

Inherent in all the training is a deep understanding of the role of the musculoskeletal system as a reciprocal factor in health and disease. Structural factors in disease processes are stressed and students are trained in osteopathic manipulative therapy as well as standard medical and surgical therapies. For further information see Useful Addresses in Chapter 9.

Why choose a DO instead of an MD?

Why indeed? If there is so little difference between the DO and the MD, why should one be chosen over the other if at all? The answer to this question lies both in the philosophy of osteopathic training and in the way that it is practised. There is an ever-increasing demand for federal funding, and if osteopathy was not different from allopathy then it would not be able to compete equally for this funding. The fact that it does compete and compete successfully means that the difference exists and is seen to exist.

From a philosophical point of view the osteopathic physician believes in the interrelationship between structure and function. He believes in the unity of the body and that both the internal and external environments have a part to play in forming the conditions that predispose a patient to disease. He asks the question 'why?' in relation to disease. 'Why this disease in this patient at this time?' He believes in the self-regulation and healing and repair systems of the body and works to

What the letters mean

AOA: American Osteopathic Association

APTA: American Physical Therapy Association

BCA: British Chiropractic Association

BNOA: British Naturopathic and Osteopathic Association

DC: Doctor of Chiropractic

DO: Diplomate in Osteopathy; Doctor of Osteopathy in USA

MACP: Manipulative Association of Chartered Physiotherapists

MCSP: Member of the Chartered Society of Physiotherapists

MLCO: Member of the London College of Osteopathy

MRO: Member of the Register of Osteopaths

OMT: Osteopathic Manipulative Therapy

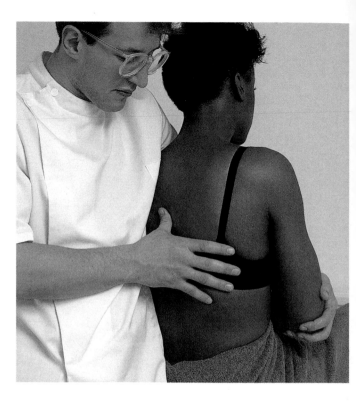

In the popular view, osteopathy means the high velocity thrust (HVT). In reality, osteopaths employ a large number of different techniques, applied after careful diagnosis of your problem.

promote this self-healing ability which is safe and free from side-effects. In all, he regards himself as a more holistic practitioner than his purely allopathic colleagues. From a practical point of view, he uses OMT in diagnosis and treatment as a basis for his work.

Osteopaths however do not simply use OMT evaluation and technique to treat disorders in the muscular system. The osteopathic cardiologist who has undergone many years of training from student days to internships and then residency programs to achieve status as a specialist may not even use manipulative skills to treat his patients. However, he does use an evaluation of the muscular system as part of his diagnostic workup in order to assess his patients more fully than if he looked at the cardiovascular system alone as part of the disease.

The end result of an osteopathic cardiologist's evaluation, then, will be a consideration of the patient, his or her heart and environment (both physical and mental) – involving the cardiovascular system and supporting systems – in order to try to find not only the tissue at fault but the fault in the tissue too.

Despite this the situation in the DO's office may differ significantly from practice to practice. Osteopathic medicine is medicine *per se*, with all the drugs and surgery that allopathic medicine has to offer and sometimes it seems that the difference between them is hard to pinpoint. If you want to be certain of consulting a practitioner who practises OMT, refer in the first instance to the American Osteopathic Association (AOA). One of their specialist colleges is the American Academy of Osteopathy whose members make a conscious effort to keep abreast of developments in OMT. Addresses are given in Chapter 9.

The American Osteopathic Association (AOA)

The AOA started in Kirksville in 1897 as the American Association for the Advancement of Osteopathy. The name changed to the AOA in 1901. It started as a group of students who were concerned about high professional standards and the legal means to protect them. They realized the need for a professional organization.

The AOA remains today the accrediting body for osteopathic education. It accredits colleges, hospitals, intern and residency syllabuses as well as postgraduate syllabuses. The Association is the authorized voice of osteopathy in the USA today. It represents the profession at local and federal level and is responsible for maintaining the integrity of the osteopathic degree without which there could be no osteopathic profession.

It is responsible for ensuring that osteopathic medicine exists as a separate entity from allopathic medicine and counters any hostility from other professional bodies towards the osteopathic profession.

The vast majority of osteopaths belong to the AOA today because they believe in the AOA as their organizing body.

Finding an osteopath

If you decide you want to consult a DO, you can find out who is practising in your state either by addressing yourself to the AOA or by consulting the Yellow Pages. Make sure that the person you choose is designated as an osteopathic physician and surgeon with the letters DO after his or her name.

Costs vary from state to state and between practitioners. Medical insurance can be arranged to cover the cost of osteopathic treatment, but you should check this before undergoing any course of treatment.

9

USEFUL
INFORMATION

GLOSSARY

Adhesion Membranes sticking together as a result of inflammation, often binding together moving surfaces such as those of JOINTS.

Angina (pectoris) Severe chest pain which may radiate down the arms; caused by shortage of oxygen in the heart muscle.

Allopathic Orthodox treatment of disease with drugs often to suppress the symptoms of that disease.

Arthritis Inflammation of a JOINT with pain and restriction of movement.
   Osteo-arthritis is a degenerative disease of larger JOINTS like the hip and knee. Rough bone deposits gradually replace CARTILAGE at the joint surfaces.

Asthma Difficulty in breathing (especially breathing out) due to narrowing of the lung bronchioles (small air passages) and accompanied by wheezing. May be caused by allergy, infection, or emotional disturbance.

Artery Strong vessel carrying oxygenated blood away from the heart. (Veins return blood to the heart.)

Bronchitis Inflammation of the small air passages of the lungs due to viral or bacterial infection.

Bunion Deformation of the joint at the base of the big toe, caused by badly fitting shoes, with a tender BURSA over the 'knuckle'.

Bursa Fluid-containing pocket of tissue that reduces friction in areas where tendons or ligaments move over bone.

Bursitis Inflammation of bursae.

Cathartic (purge) A strong laxative drug which induces opening of the bowels.

Colic Intermittent, frequently severe pain caused by strong contractions of involuntary muscles which stretch the nerve endings of internal organs; caused by inflammation or obstruction.

Constipation Failure of waste matter in the large intestine to find its way to the rectum and/or failure of a bowel movement to completely empty the rectum of waste. It is not an important illness in itself but may sometimes be a symptom of more serious illness.

Diarrhoea Frequent and often uncontrollable passage of watery bowel movements.

Degeneration Alteration of body cells towards cell types with less specialized functions, often caused by infection or inefficient blood supply.

Down's Syndrome Also called mongolism. A congenital defect of mental and physical development. People with Down's Syndrome have 47 chromosomes instead of the normal 46 in their body cells. Those affected are mentally handicapped to a greater or lesser extent; physically they are usually short, with flat round faces, a fold of skin over the inner corner of the eye and straight hair.

Dysfunction Failure of an organ or system to function normally.

Emphysema A condition of the lungs where the small air spaces (alveoli) become over-inflated and lose their dividing walls. There is progressive deterioration of lung function, with constant coughing, difficulty breathing and shortness of breath. Often a sequel to chronic BRONCHITIS.

Flatulence Gas in the stomach and intestine which causes discomfort. Most of the air is swallowed; some is produced by fermentation in the lower intestine, especially if a person is constipated.

Haemorrhoids (piles) Varicose veins at the junction of the rectum and the anal canal just above the anal opening. Haemorrhoids bleed and are itchy and uncomfortable. No single cause but very common in pregnant women because the pelvic veins become compressed.

Hamstring muscles The group of long, thin strap muscles at the back of the thigh which flex the knee and help extend the hip.

Hypermobility Excessive mobility (of a JOINT).

Hypomobility Too little mobility (of a JOINT).

Joints There are two sorts of joints in the human body: mobile or synovial joints and fixed or fibrous joints.
The body has more synovial joints than fibrous. Where bones meet, the ends of each are enclosed in a thick fibrous capsule which is lined with synovial membrane. This secretes synovial fluid to lubricate the bones as they move against each other.
Fibrous joints do not allow movement between bones. The bones of the skull are bonded together with fibrous tissue.

Lesion Disturbance of the function or structure of a part of the body, as with a wound or tumour.

Ligament Fibrous band between two bones at a joint. A ligament is flexible but cannot stretch. Ligaments set the limits beyond which movement is impossible. Any intermediate position of a JOINT is held entirely by muscles. If a JOINT is forced beyond its normal range the ligament will tear: this is called a sprain.

Lumbar Concerning the part of the back between the lowest pair of ribs and the top of the PELVIS.

Lymph Colourless fluid which is squeezed out from the body's smallest blood vessels, the capillaries. It washes through the body's tissues, flushing out waste matter, cell debris and

bacteria, eventually draining into the LYMPHATIC SYSTEM.

Lymphatic system A one-way network of drainage channels which receives debris laden LYMPH as it washes through the body tissues. At various points in the system, notably the neck, groin and armpit, there are groups of lymph nodes. These filter off the waste matter and destroy it. They also manufacture some of the antibodies and white blood cells which form the body's defence system. Swollen lymph nodes, which are visible outside the body and can often be felt as local discomfort, are a sign that your body is dealing with an infection by producing more antibodies.

Mastoiditis Infection and inflammation of the mastoid bone behind the ear; usually follows from middle ear infection and can lead to deafness.

Meningitis A dangerous condition where the membranes (*meninges*) covering the brain and spinal cord become inflamed due to viral or bacterial infection.

Migraine A recurring condition of severe headaches usually accompanied by dizziness, nausea and impaired vision.

Multiple sclerosis A chronic condition of the central nervous system in which small areas of the brain and spinal cord degenerate.

Neuralgia A pain originating in a nerve (eg SCIATICA).

Neurology The study of nerves and the nervous system and its disorders. Hence neurological – to do with nerves and the nervous system.

Obstetrics Medical care and treatment during pregnancy and childbirth.

Orthodontics Correction of naturally badly positioned teeth and/or misaligned jaw.

Osteoporosis (brittle bones) Thinning and weakening of the bones, usually in old age, largely due to calcium loss. It is more common in women than men after the menopause.

Pelvis The strong girdle of bone which gives stability to the lower part of the body. It consists of the *sacrum* (the five lowest vertebrae of the spine fused together to make one solid bone) and two hip bones. Each hip bone has three parts: the *ischium* or rump; the *ilium* which supports the sides of the abdomen; and at the front the *pubis*. The pubis of each hip meet at the front of the body, and are bound together by tough fibrous tissue.

Pharmacopoeia List of approved drugs with notes on their dosage, purity, and preparation.

Pharmacology Scientific study and research of drugs.

GLOSSARY

Physiotherapy   Treatment of illness by physical means such as exercise, massage, heat and electricity. It aims to relieve pain in joints and maintain and restore limb function after injury.

Placebo   Medication-free remedy given to patients who believe that it contains drugs which will help them get better. Trials show that 75% of people on placebos show a marked degree of improvement.

Podiatrist   Chiropodist.

Referred pain   Pain felt in a different part of the body from the originating site of the infection or injury.

Somatic   Relating to muscles, ligaments and bones.

Spasm   Involuntary contraction of a muscle or LIGAMENT, usually sudden and painful. It can be instant or prolonged.

Symptom   Physical or mental change indicating the presence of disorder or disease in the body.

Tendon   An extremely tough fibrous cord joining a muscle to a bone.

Thorax   Often referred to as 'chest'. The compartment of the body enclosed by the ribs, from the first rib to the diaphragm at the bottom.

Tinnitus   Hissing, buzzing or ringing sounds in the ear, caused by disorders of the ear or its nerve.

Torsion   Twisting.

Trauma   Physical or mental injury. Physical trauma (damage to tissues) can be caused by cuts, blows, burns, etc.

Traction   Continuous or intermittent pull on a limb or body part during treatment.

Vascular   Of vessels, particularly the blood vessels.

Vertigo   Dizziness, with a feeling of whirling and loss of contact with the earth. Caused by a disturbed sense of balance.

Visceral   Relating to the internal organs of the thorax (heart, lungs) and the abdominal cavity (stomach, intestines, liver, spleen, kidneys).

USEFUL ADDRESSES

Osteopathy

UK
The General Council and Register of Osteopaths (GCRO)
21 Suffolk Street, London SW1Y 4HG

British Naturopathic and Osteopathic Association
Frazer House, 6 Netherall Gardens,
London NW3 5RR

British School of Osteopathy (BSO)
Littlejohn House, 1-4 Suffolk Street,
London SW1Y 4HG

European School of Osteopathy
104 Tonbridge Road, Maidstone,
Kent ME16 8SL

Osteopathic Association Clinic
8 Boston Place, London NW1

USA
American Osteopathic Association (AOA)
142 East Ontario, Chicago, Illinois 60611

American Academy of Osteopathy
PO Box 750, 12 West Locust St, Newark, Ohio 43055

The Cranial Academy
1140 West 8th Street, Meridian,
ID 83642

There are several osteopathic colleges in most States. For a list of those in your State, apply to the dept. of education (Dr Ward's office) at the AOA, Chicago.

Australia
Australian Osteopathic Association
551 Hampton Street, Hampton, Victoria 3188

Canada
Canadian Osteopathic Association
575 Waterloo Street, London, Ontario

New Zealand
Register of New Zealand Osteopaths
c/o Robert Bowden, 92 Hurstmere Road, Takapuna,
Auckland

Other Organizations UK

British Medical Association (BMA)
British Medical Association House,
Tavistock Square, London WC1

Chartered Society of Physiotherapists
14 Bedford Row, London WC1R 4ED

Council for Complementary & Alternative Medicine (CCAM)
Suite 1, 19a Cavendish Square, London W1M 9AD

Institute for Complementary Medicine (ICM)
21 Portland Place, London W1N 3AF

Other Organizations USA

American Medical Association
535 North Deerborn Street, Chicago, Illinois 60610

American Physical Therapy Association
1111 North Fairfax Street, Alexandria,
Virginia 22314

American Holistic Medical Association
2727 Fairview Avenue East, Seattle,
Washington 98102

National Foundation for Holistic Medicine
66 Milton Road, Rye, New York 10580

FURTHER READING

Osteopathy

Leon Chaitow
Osteopathy: head-to-toe health through manipulation
Thorsons, Wellingborough 1977

Osteopathy: a complete health care system
Thorsons, Wellingborough 1982

George W Northup
Osteopathic Medicine: An American Reformation
American Osteopathy Association, Chicago 1979

Leon E Page
Osteopathic Fundamentals
Tamor Pierston, London 1981

Reginald Wier Puttick
Osteopathy
Faber, London 1956

Stephen Sandler
Osteopathy
Optima, London 1987

Alan Stoddard
Manual of Osteopathic Techniques
Hutchinson, London 1980

Edward Triance
Osteopathy: A Patient's Guide
Thorsons, Wellingborough 1986

General

Boston Women's Health Collective
(Angela Phillips and Jill Rakusen eds)
Our Bodies, Our Selves
Penguin/Boston Women's Collective 1978

Fritjof Capra
The Turning Point
Fontana, London 1983

Dr S J Fulder
A Handbook of Complementary Medicine
Coronet Books, London 1984

Ann Hill (ed.)
A Visual Encyclopedia of Unconventional Medicine
New English Library, London 1979

Ivan Illich
Limits to Medicine: Medical Nemesis
Calder & Boyars
London 1976; Penguin 1977

Brian Inglis
The Diseases of Civilization
Hodder & Stoughton, London 1981

Brian Inglis and Ruth West
The Alternative Health Guide·
Michael Joseph/Mermaid, London 1983

Leslie K Kaslof (ed.)
Holistic Dimensions in Healing: A Resource Guide
Doubleday, New York 1978

Gerald Kogan (ed.)
Your Body Works: A Guide to Health, Energy and Balance
Transform, Berkeley, California 1980

E K Ledermann
Good Health through Natural Therapy
Kogan Page, London 1976

Patrick C Pietroni
Holistic Medicine: Old Map, New Territory
British Journal of Holistic Medicine, vol 1, London 1984

Richard Totman
Social Causes of Illness
Souvenir Press, London 1979

Michael van Straten
The Natural Health Consultant
Ebury Press, London 1987

INDEX

INDEX

INDEX

ACKNOWLEDGMENTS

The publishers would like to thank the following organizations and individuals for their kind permission to reproduce the illustrations in this book:

ACE Photo Agency: 17/R. Howard 13/M. Bluestone 27/G. Palmer 51 **American Osteopathic Association:** 139 **BBC Hulton Picture Library:** 137 **Ian Christy Photography:** 49 **Greg Evans Photo Library:** 73 **Mary Evans Picture Library:** 133, 134 **General Council and Register of Osteopaths:** 38, 39, 41, 42, 43, 45, 46, 79, 84, 86, 151 **Popperfoto:** 9 **Ann Ronan Picture Library:** 131, 135 **Science Photo Library/Heini Schneebeli:** 128 **Stephen Sandler:** 103 left and right **Sporting Pictures (UK) Ltd.:** 52 **Tony Stone Associates:** 14, 18, 126 **Thorsons Publishing Group Ltd.:** 119 **John Watney:** 122 **Zefa:** 99 right

The following photographs were specially taken by **Peter Chadwick:** 6, 7, 10, 16, 20, 22, 25, 28 above & below, 54, 61 above & below, 67, 68, 69, 78, 81, 83, 93, 94, 95, 96, 97 above & below, 98, 99 left, 101, 102, 106, 108, 109, 116, 120, 144, 148, 150

Our thanks to the **Westminster Natural Health Centre, London** for their help with these photographs.

Illustrations   Elaine Anderson

Editor Viv Croot   **Art Editor** Alyson Kyles
Coordinating Editor Camilla Simmons   **Designer** Malcolm Smythe
Production Alyssum Ross   **Picture Research** Christina Weir